BAGHDAD BUSINESS SCHOOL

Heyrick Bond Gunning

BAGHDAD BUSINESS SCHOOL

The Challenges of a War Zone Start Up

Heyrick Bond Gunning

Published by Eye Books

Baghdad Business School
First Edition
September 2004

Published by Eye Books Ltd
51a Boscombe Rd
London
W12 9HT
Tel/fax: +44 (0) 20 8743 3276
website: www.eye-books.com

Set in Frutiger and Garamond
ISBN: 1903070333

British Library Cataloguing in Publication Data
A catalogue record for this book is available from the British Library

Printed and bound in Great Britain by Biddles Ltd

Cover photograph courtesy of Jennifer Glasse

To Anna

Acknowledgements

To Phil Armatage who was there from the start and who helped me retain my sanity and humour. To Dominic Herbert and Zaid for contributing with their insightful pieces. To all at DHL Iraq for working so successfully under such difficult conditions, in particular John Chisholm for his unrelenting support. To the Bahrain office, notably Phil Couchman, Fiona, Breda and Harsha for helping to make the operation run more smoothly. Finally, to Dan, Chris and Mark for all their hard work in helping to put this book together.

Contents

MAP OF IRAQ

INTRODUCTION

Do we need another book about Iraq? It often doesn't feel like it. The conflict and attempted reconstruction have already produced suffocating media coverage. The political intensity - the fading pretext for invasion - has charged it all with a wearying combativeness. It has become numbing and feels increasingly stale. And the effect has been to drive us towards an indifference about the detail of its human dimension. The mainstream story is no longer about the people on the ground, the Iraqis, the soldiers, the legions of non-Iraqis providing support services or mining the security gold rush. It has become preoccupied with the degree of blame for all its ugliness that can be thrown at George Bush, Tony Blair, and the suppliers of their alleged intelligence. All these might combine to argue for a pause for breath. But it is the alienating distortion of the story that makes another book so important, something that turns our attention back to the human elements.

The value of Baghdad Business School lies in this freshness, both its concern with the micro rather than the macro and its unique perspective on post-war Iraq. Heyrick is not a journalist, a politician, aid worker or soldier (any more). He is a businessman and has a voice and an interest in the country that we haven't yet heard. His experiences were not about policy or politics. They were about the mundane and maddening frustrations of trying to set up a business in a country undergoing the trauma of post-totalitarianism.

None of the agendas that underlie everything else we have seen or read or heard to date. His worries were inevitably about security but they were also about air-conditioning units, finding people to work for him, how to get a drink and the etiquette of ten-pin bowling. He had employees to motivate and a civilian job to do. And most importantly, he interacted with Iraqis not as an occupier or liberator but as the boss of a big postal company.

Therein lies another immense value in Heyrick's story. Turning it around and reflecting it upon the more conventional business experience produces a joyful antidote to the epic pretension of most management theorising. No flow charts, two-by-two matrices, or clever financial models. This was just getting the job done without the luxury of time to pontificate or wallow in vacuous meetings. It was no frills business, the Land Rover school of supply chain management. Heyrick's success in setting up his outfit and leaving a working legacy is testament to his composure, pragmatism, courage and wit. And it's the wit that will probably be the most engaging feature of this chronicle. It is infused with a charm and warmth and a thread of gentle English eccentricity that has long been in short supply.

1 PLANNING A CAREER

Planning a successful career requires a great deal of thought and attention. Once the general career path has been identified it is essential to review all the major participants, understand their strengths and weaknesses, and narrow down the range of possibilities. Approach the firms that both suit your medium and long-term ambitions and are culturally sympathetic. Conduct a form of due diligence on them all to be prepared for any ensuing dialogue. This is no time for being impulsive - you are choosing a family as much as an employer.

(The Encyclopedia of Current Business Orthodoxy)

Monday morning, the first day back at work, after three weeks spent on a wonderful holiday in New Zealand. The phone rang, breaking my reverie and I could feel myself slipping back into the routine as if I had never been away. The next nine words were to metamorphose my rather staid existence. 'Are you interested in setting up DHL in Iraq?' The caller, an ex colleague of mine, went on to explain that DHL was looking for someone with military and commercial experience and was keen to interview me. My initial reaction was to feel flattered, quickly followed by doubts over whether the firm had called the right man. Had DHL mistaken a rather normal career in the army for something else or had they seen one of my recently written CVs extolling my virtues as a major mover in the world of mergers and acquisitions?! In truth I had left the Grenadier Guards three years previously. Whilst in the army I had spent some time in London wearing a tunic and bearskin, carrying out public duties. As with most soldiers, I had then spent more time than I intended in Northern Ireland but was fortunate to have worked in a more unusual role which made it a little more exciting than normal soldiering. I had left the army and thought I had fallen on my feet working in a start up. My timing was impeccable - 'Mergermarket' was a Financial Services dotcom - and I joined just as the dotcom bubble burst and the bottom fell out of the M&A market. But Mergermarket dropped the .com and went on to thrive, giving me the commercial experience DHL now found so appealing. Following an hour or two of stalling I made up my mind to go out to Bahrain for an interview.

I didn't want anyone at work to know for the obvious reasons and also in case they thought I had lost the plot entirely. Timing was key and I managed to get a flight on Tuesday night. It enabled me to get to Bahrain for Wednesday morning, have my interviews that day and be back at my desk by seven on Thursday morning, having made a miraculous recovery from my supposed bout of ill health. As it turned out the two sleepless nights meant I looked less than well and no one thought to challenge my absence. The flight out had been interesting. It was the first day of Gulf War II and unsurprisingly there were not many takers for the Gulf Air flight to Bahrain. The flight attendants outnumbered the six of us who rattled around the plane. I stretched out on a row of seats, sipped some champagne and read my notes on DHL.

I had done some rather hurried research earlier in the day that ran short of finding out what the D, H & L stood for. What I did know was that it was a courier company founded by three lawyers in 1969. It had recently been bought by Deutsche Post and was keen to increase their influence in the Middle East by adding Iraq to the list of 147 countries in which it already operated.

Bahrain is an interesting place. I had never been to the Middle East before but it is clear to the casual observer that money is no object when it comes to impressing the visitor or your countrymen. The easiest way to do this is through building and owning a bigger/taller hotel or office block than the largest most recently built version. The result is a series of tall glass buildings scattered around the island. The hotel I checked into was one of these and was unintentionally retro and kitsch. Anything that is big, shiny and obvious is all the rage; understated was removed from the dictionary years ago. It was also apparent that walking was not something one was expected to do. I had wandered down to a mall that turned out to be devoid of shoppers. This was for good reason, as many of the shops were being refitted, so after a cursory glance around I moved on to a second mall that was 50m away. There was simply no footpath, but there was a taxi waiting to take me there. Being a tight tourist and never one to take the easy option, I ended up dashing across four lanes of traffic and with a policeman in hot pursuit I ran up the slip road, avoiding the oncoming traffic and into the next mall. I had a quick look at some watches that were drowning in diamonds, and then walked back to the hotel. On my return journey I was struck by the number of non-Arabs there were working in the country. They provide much of the manual labour and many can be found cutting the grass in the central reservation or painting lines on the roads. As they progress along the road there is invariably an unlucky soul with a traffic cone tied to a long piece of string around his waist. He acts as the warning to approaching traffic and slowly drags his cone behind him, in the wake of the grass cutters and line painters. It is sights like this and a look down the back streets, behind the shiny façade, that reminds one that beneath this rather sterile exterior lies a vibrant Middle Eastern culture. The main thoroughfares are so clean that I actually saw a guy sponging down the back of a road sign!

I headed back to the airport for my interviews and met several directors, had lunch in a hotel and returned for more interviews in the afternoon. The only point at which I almost came unstuck was when asked what DHL stood for; I knew I had not researched this but I also knew that there was an answer in me somewhere. I remembered that as I had approached the interview room I had walked past three conference rooms called Dalsey, Hillblom and Lynn. My embarrassment was spared. The interview went well and mentally I started planning my stay in Bahrain, waiting for the war to end and the Coalition to grant commercial entities permission to enter the country. The day ended with a swim and a couple of beers before boarding the plane back to UK. The flight back was the antithesis of the outward journey. I was surprised the plane managed to get off the ground. I had forgotten there was a war going on in Iraq, prompting a mass exodus from Bahrain and people boarding the plane with glorious quantities of hand luggage.

Following some negotiations over the remuneration, I spent a week wrestling with the decision over whether or not to accept the job. So why did I say yes? This is a difficult one to answer. I had just got engaged, my job was going well and I had the opportunity to go and set up the New York office for Mergermarket. Long discussions ensued and I decided that it really was too good an opportunity to let slip through my fingers. It is not often that one is handed an opportunity to do something that is so potentially life changing. There were also other drivers that explained my decision. I have a joint honours in The Geography of International Business and Archaeology and had specialised in the Middle East. I had a romantic view of going to visit the archaeological sites that I had never really expected to be able to see. Iraq is the birthplace of modern civilization. I viewed the opening of Iraq as a moment in history and I desperately wanted to be a part of it. Subconsciously I think the fact that I had many friends who were a part of the Coalition Forces probably brought out the competitive streak in me. Without trying to sound trite, I did feel that I was missing out on an adventure. I was envious of my friends in the armed forces who were spearheading the move into Iraq. Although I had obviously missed that particular boat I could envisage future conversations with military friends; 'I admit the war may have been dangerous but try setting up a business in a war torn country with little support.' To many it may sound strange but to me it was obvious that when given the choice of setting up an office in New York or setting up a countrywide network in Iraq, the latter was a clear favourite. The fact that I was entering the unknown in terms of the logistics business and in terms of the environment simply added to the appeal. I handed in my notice. Before I left work I sent a quick email to a few clients thanking them for their support and explaining that I was off to Baghdad. I invited them to visit me if they were in the region. The email was picked up by the Evening Standard and read as follows:

"HEYRICK Bond-Gunning, former Grenadier Guards officer turned manager for M&A website Mergermarket.com, has sent the following email to clients 'After a few fantastic years, I am leaving Mergermarket, having accepted the offer of a job to set up DHL in Iraq. Thank you for being an excellent set of clients and I hope our paths cross in the future. If you happen to be passing through Baghdad, please email me.' I gather this is not an April fool but that the fellow is actually looking forward to the new challenge. It seems unlikely though that the clients will be quite as keen as Heyrick to stay in touch."

Following numerous farewell parties, it was suddenly the morning of my departure. I found myself standing over an empty suitcase struggling over the decisions of what to pack. I had been told to expect at least a week in Bahrain whilst we waited for permission to enter Iraq. On getting into the country we would probably be based at the airport, not the local Hilton but in the Baghdad equivalent - a tent. Suits and tents don't really go hand in hand but then I also had visions of waiting in Bahrain for the coalition forces to finish their job in Iraq. So in went a suit and some shirts, lots of t-shirts and anything linen I could lay may hands on. It was already 40 degrees in Iraq and it was due to reach the mid 50s in the summer. This was a worry. I am not known for my tolerance of anything above 30, so 40 made my face go red just thinking about it. I found the best way to deal with that particular concern was to stop thinking about it and concentrate on finding some shorts. Next dilemma, tennis racket, golf clubs or neither? Now could be the chance I had been waiting for to actually take the clubs out of their rather expensive bag. I had visions of driving a ball down an empty runway but then realized that there may be issues with aircraft and actually it wouldn't have looked so professional if I arrived to set up a business clutching a couple of tennis rackets and some clubs. I decided on three clubs and the tennis rackets, all of which fitted into my bag. The remainder of the space was filled with plenty of sun cream, a roll up Panama, some files, a compass, a gas mask, a bulletproof jacket and some Arabic language tapes. It was at this point that I had a slight reality check. I was not going to be wearing a flak jacket over a suit so the suit stayed in London. I wondered what an earth I was letting myself in for.

I had done a fair amount of research since accepting the job and although most of the information predated the first Gulf War, I had been able to write a draft strategy paper. Amongst other things, it contained a guide on survival in hostile environments that I had cobbled together. I re-read it, twice, had a beer and felt less concerned. I had also spoken to various family friends who had experienced the Middle East, working with Arabs and in one case with Iraqis. I gleaned some remarkable information from a family friend who had often worked in Iraq. On his last trip he had been incarcerated by Saddam and had remained in jail for ten years. You would think that he was not the ideal man to inspire me with confidence but he did not have a bad thing to say about the Iraqis. He explained that the majority were well educated, to degree level. He added that they were a naturally open and hospitable people and were extremely interested in what went on in the west. On the work front, he warned me that they enjoyed a good haggle but that once they had agreed a deal they would stick to it. However, if they could find a loophole or short cut they had a tendency to feel that it was their duty to exploit it. A firm but fair approach was advised when dealing with employees.

The next question was the language. Many Iraqis speak a little English, but I realised that a smattering of Arabic would help. I had invested in the cassettes and started learning the basic vocabulary. I also worked on a healthy amount of contacts to meet up with whilst waiting in Bahrain. Despite these preparations, I did have a real feeling that I was going into the unknown and a far from friendly environment. I had seen pictures of dead and wounded civilians and was worried how Iraqis might respond even if the Coalition kept the collateral damage to a minimum. Would they think I was there to exploit them? Would they view me as an extension of the Coalition Forces? Would they welcome me or would their pride and unfulfilled expectations mean they would resent me? I suspected it would be a combination of all of these feelings and that I was going to have to be very aware of the mood of the people, their expectations and their culture. I also realised that I could sit and ponder over these questions ad infinitum and decided that the only way they were going to be answered was by getting out there. I was as ready as I was ever going to be and following some painful farewells, boarded the flight to Bahrain.

2 DEVELOPING A BUSINESS PLAN

Developing a business plan in readiness to enter a new market requires thorough market research, an understanding of the incumbents, and a strategy that will make an immediate impact. The greater the detail of your plan, the better equipped you will be to respond to the inevitable surprises you encounter on launch.

(The Encyclopedia of Current Business Orthodoxy).

A bleary eyed arrival at 6.30 a.m. saw me met by an even more tired looking taxi driver. I gave him the address for the office and asked him how much it was going to cost. 'Whatever you wish' was the reply. Not really in the mood for smart arsed comments I hit back with a joke price and he simply rolled his eyes, having heard it all before. I was putty in his hands, we drove the half-mile to the office and he fleeced me at the other end. It did however remind me that the Arabs like to bargain over everything, enjoying the whole process and this was something I was going to have to get used to. I arrived at the office and began to mentally prepare myself for a day of brainstorming over the business strategy for Iraq. I was soon to be reminded that sometimes planning is overrated, as I went straight into a briefing to be told that I shouldn't bother checking into my hotel but that I was to board another plane for Baghdad. The Coalition had given us permission to fly and so DHL was going to be the first commercial flight into Iraq since the end of the war.

I went to help load the plane and met Phil Armatage, the colleague with whom I was to work in Iraq. He had worked for DHL for a few years and he was to prove vital in filling the gaps in my knowledge about how the DHL systems were supposed to operate. My initial impression was of a brusque Geordie, but I was soon to find out that he was often able to reveal a more sensitive side, particularly whilst in pursuit of love! Phil had flown into Bahrain the previous day and we both went to board the plane and have a look at the supplies we had been given. On climbing into the body of the Antonov 12 we were met with a sight that caused considerable laughter. It was clear that little thought had gone into the planning. Sitting in front of us were two vehicles, a Land Rover Discovery and a canary yellow van with DHL on its side. The former was ideal but the latter was a joke. I was damned if I was going to drive around Baghdad in a vehicle that was just asking to be looted. Before we had even taken off we had already decided that it was going to be used on the airport only, where it would probably act as a very good advert to the US Forces that were based there. I threw open the doors of the van to look at our supplies. It was empty. We had a look in the back of the Landrover and it was then that a wave of concern hit me. We were woefully under prepared. The list of kit and equipment was as follows:

2 camp beds
1 satellite phone
1 laptop
1 tent
1 Tupperware box with baked beans, soup and corned beef
24 Bottles of water
1 x envelope containing $25000

That was it. I couldn't have written a more ridiculous scenario if I had tried. Not really what one would expect to set up a multi million dollar business with but I suppose it was a start.

I realised that DHL Middle East had been caught by surprise by the sudden permission to fly; so with a shrug of the shoulders and a smile we got over our initial surprise and boarded the aircraft. The plane, about 35 years old, used to belong to the Russian air force and was piloted by some large hairy Bulgarians. The plane was manned by a crew of seven. Inside the cockpit were the two pilots, an engineer behind them and a navigator sitting in the nose with a set of binoculars. There were then three more crew who played a wide range of roles from engineers, to loadmasters and tea makers. Once in the air, they revealed that a few months earlier they had misjudged their landing into Bagram airfield, Afghanistan and ended up overshooting the runway and grinding to a halt in a minefield. The air traffic controller told them to stay put to which they replied 'no problem,' turned the plane around in the minefield, and then drove out! I was not inspired with confidence. Needless to say, true to form, they managed to fly at the wrong altitude as we entered Iraq. Two US F16s were scrambled to intercept us. An image of me adorned with a Tom Hanks like beard whilst stranded in the middle of the desert flashed through my mind. Fortunately with DHL painted on the side of the plane we were escorted rather than dispatched.

The flight over also gave me a chance to think about how the business was going to develop. I was no longer going to have the luxury of a week in Bahrain getting to know the business but Phil's expertise had that particular problem covered. We were lacking basic equipment and I drew up a short list of what we required at the top of which was a satellite link for the email. In spite of these minor practical issues we were in the fortunate position of starting from scratch, with very few preconceptions and the support of a global business. I underpinned my plan by using the structure of a military template that I had utilised to help solve problems in the past. I may not have had much immediate preparedness but at least my previous experiences had equipped me with a model I could apply to even the most uncertain environment. I asked myself a series of questions and this helped me to work out how we might develop the business in its initial stages. At every stage, the outcomes were tested further by questions that ultimately produced a series of tasks. And these tasks were then explored according to their feasibility.

1. MISSION ANALYSIS
   - Mission - state the mission and look at mission verbs. Deconstruct the sentence and look at exactly what it is you are required to do.
   - What was the intent of my boss/what is my role in the plan?
   - Tasks - these take two forms, those that are

specified and those that are implied or you feel would help you achieve your mission.

- Constraints/freedoms - are there any freedoms or constraints that I need to be aware of?
- Review the scenario - have the parameters changed since I was first given the mission?
- Timeline - draw a timeline as this helps picture deadlines.

2. FACTORS - ENVIRONMENT
- Geography - what/where are the major cities? What is the transport network like? What are the communications networks like? What is the weather like?
- History - a brief look at the history of a country helps explain how and why people react in certain ways.
- Religion - what are the various religious groups and what are the salient differentials with each group?
- Ethnic groups - who are the key political figures? How can I get DHL in front of them?
- Work ethic - what is the business etiquette? Have western work practices been utilised in the country?
- Health - what is the general health of the population? Are the hospitals of a good standard? Are we going to be able to use the hospitals if needs be?

3. FACTORS - ENEMY (COMPETITION)
- Vital ground/key terrain - vital ground refers to the parts of the business that are vital for our survival. Key terrain is the parts of the business

that would give us a significant advantage over our competition.

- Enemy disposition - are there any competitors in the market already? If so, how many are there, who are their main clients, what is their offering and how does it compare to ours?
- Threat evaluation - enemy strengths and weaknesses. What are they good at and what are they bad at?
- Enemy approaches - how are the competition going to be entering the market place?

4. FACTORS - FRIENDLY FORCES (OWN ASSETS / ALLIANCES)
- Own assets - what assets do I have at my disposal?
- Alliances - are there any third party alliances I need to be aware of?
- Strengths - what are my strengths?
- Weaknesses - what are my weaknesses?

5. FACTORS - SECURITY AND SURPRISE
- Operational security - is the environment safe to work in? How can I limit the risk? Is my competitive advantage sustainable if I keep my operational recipe secret?
- Deception - will deception help limit the threat? Will this also make our model more difficult for a competitor to replicate?

6. ASSESSMENT OF TASKS
- List the tasks that come out of the above process and allocate the resources to each task.

7. COURSES OF ACTION

- A comparison of the courses of action in a table as follows:

	COA1		COA2		COA3	
Criteria	+ve	-ve	+ve	-ve	+ve	-ve

8. PLAN

- Select a Course of Action and now concentrate on the way in which this is going to be implemented. Prepare to be flexible as no plan can take account of unforeseen factors that will influence it down the line. Remember, however well prepared you are few plans maintain their format even in the initial stages of implementation.

3 NETWORKING

Getting to know people in your immediate professional environment is imperative. They are a source of information and opportunity. Everyone is of value even if it is sometimes a challenge to determine just how that value can be extracted. The corollary is that everyone should be treated with respect in an effort to develop lasting relationships. This is more generally known as networking.

(The Encyclopedia of Current Business Orthodoxy)

The plane gave a violent shudder as the wheels were cranked out of the undercarriage and I had a reality check. I could strategise to my heart's content but before anything was going to happen I needed to find out where we would be sleeping that night. I had visions of snuggling up next to Phil in the back of the DHL banana van. He seemed a nice enough guy but it was not what I really had in mind when I had been told I would be working closely with him.

On landing at Saddam International Airport, as the first civilian flight in since the war, we were surrounded by a protective cordon of troops. They stared at us, mouths wide open as we bade them 'good morning' and promptly drove the bright yellow DHL van out onto the tarmac. We did a bit of back slapping, took some cheesy photos, and then met the military. It was at this point that networking took on a completely different meaning. In my book there are now two types. Type A involves networking for your own survival and type B is the business variety. The first thing to do was to find as many people with guns and go and introduce ourselves to them - definitely type A. Having got over our total disregard for the tactical situation, they couldn't have been more welcoming. We were to discover later that this was because they had been in the Middle East since August. They had overstretched their conversational limits with each other and were quite keen for some fresh chat. I stopped and had a look around. The initial excitement of being the first into the airport was wearing off rapidly. I was standing on the apron, next to the runway. Behind me was a cargo hangar, riddled with bullet holes and open to the elements on one side. This was probably going to be my home for the foreseeable future. The upside was that I wasn't going to be in a tent.

With the plane unloaded and photo mission accomplished, the various directors gave us hearty handshakes and with unashamed joy got back into the plane. As the plane rumbled down the runway I did wonder when I would next be seeing civilisation. I used my satellite phone for the first time and made a call to a friend who I knew would be impressed with my location and tried to persuade him that he should come and join me as it was really good fun. I then called my fiancé, Anna, who was not nearly as impressed but quite relieved. It was 40 degrees and I was standing on a runway at Saddam International Airport, my bag at my feet and a bulging wallet stuffed into my pocket. For a moment I was slightly dazed as I watched my link to civilisation disappear towards the horizon, belching huge clouds of black smoke as they went.

Gunfire rattled in the distance and plumes of smoke could be seen drifting from the ruins of buildings so we quickly went into the hangar, lugging our bags and meagre supplies. The hangar was huge, two football pitches huge. It was also full of rubbish, old Iraqi Airways paperwork, bits of aircraft and ground handling equipment in various degrees of disrepair. This had been piling up for a while because it was on every single shelf. A layer of dust and sand covered every surface because half of the front of the warehouse had been shot off and the remainder was like a sieve. The space was split down the middle by a two floor office block that ran the width of the hangar and contained about 20 rooms. As we grew bolder, our priority rapidly changed from befriending people with guns to finding a place to stay. The office block looked like a good place to start and concierge lacking, we wandered off to find ourselves a room. We found that, most of the doors had been blown off by the marines and those that weren't, had huge holes where the handles had been. For good measure there were then various holes in the ceiling. We picked a room at random and set up our camp beds in a corner and locked the rest of our belongings in the car. We even managed to find some rather gaudy furniture and a rug that had been borrowed from one of the palaces near the airport. A further wander around the hangar made me realize how lucky we were with our room as every other one contained piles of broken office furniture and several piles of shit, the calling card of the Marines. They were so full of junk it was clear that no real work had been done there in the past few years, despite it being the only commercial freight-handling hangar on the airport. It was as if things ground to a standstill post Gulf War I.

So there we were, staying in an old aircraft hangar with some liberated carpets thrown on the floor. These, we discovered, came from one of Saddam's 52 palaces. We heard amazing stories about what had been found by the first troops. The airport contained two particularly interesting hangars. The first was crammed to the rafters with duty free - after shaves, perfumes and alcohol - most of which were also liberated by the coalition forces. More impressive however was a second hangar containing what was reputed to be Uday's private car collection. Every and any marque you could care to mention was there. We were told that they burnt the lot but I wouldn't be surprised if there are a few Ferraris being driven around Texas that could tell an interesting tale.

The soldiers made amusing company for a while, once we overcame the initial hurdle; we were asked what language was spoken in England. It was clear that most of them had never left the US and when one commented that all he had learnt about other cultures was what he'd read in the bible, I realised things may be a bit of an uphill struggle. It was time to make an exit, so we decided to take a trip out of the airport and find out what was going on in Baghdad. This was particularly exciting, as we had specifically been told to wait and see how things developed before we started driving around. Our view was that we were going to see nothing inside a hangar and that we were actually there to set up a business. We decided to head for what we perceived to be the hub of Baghdad, the Palestine Hotel. We only knew about this because it was the one where a journalist had unfortunately been killed as a result of some friendly fire during the war. I consulted my 1989 tourist map and was interested to see that there were also a few bars and nightclubs on the banks of the Tigris. So, full of hope, we set off in search of the hotel.

The airport is only about 25 minutes away from the centre of town. As we drove along we noticed huge holes in the wall surrounding the airport where it had been breached by tanks. There was an excellent road in, providing you avoided the burnt out vehicle wrecks and the potholes caused by various munitions. Another obstacle was the children that lay in wait at the side of the road. As our car approached them they would make a suicidal dash at the car, hands outstretched, asking for food and money. I made a mental note to bring a bag of army rations with me the next time we ventured into town. Dotted along the roads at regular intervals, I noticed there were what could be best described as large metal sun umbrellas. We later learned that this was where members of Saddam's secret police used to stand, in the shadows, just watching. Watching to report on anyone that was seen on this restricted road or anything that involved Iraqi interaction with a foreigner, as both were strictly forbidden.

I didn't really know what to expect in Baghdad. I thought it wouldn't have been in too bad a state as the Coalition Forces were using precision bombing. As it turned out their bombing had indeed been precise, there had just been rather a lot of it. Most of the tall buildings, barring the hotels, had holes in them and there was a thick layer of dust that covered the city. In the run up to the war the people had realized that there would probably be a regime change and had begun to appropriate what they could lay their hands on. For example it was not uncommon to see airport vehicles with Iraqi Airways written on the side, driving through the city. The chaos was increased when Saddam opened all the prisons and mental institutions, releasing the inmates. The end of the war heralded a tremendous physical and mental release for the Iraqis and this manifested itself in widespread rioting and indiscriminate looting. During the rioting almost all of the supermarkets were destroyed by Iraqis. But having spoken to them I was informed that some of this was carefully targeted and was at the behest of those that wanted to get rid of the competition. This rang true as some supermarkets had remained remarkably unscathed. The principle targets were the much hated Palaces and these were looted by all and sundry, including some journalists. I met one who had found a photo album of Saddam's and had sold it to Paris Match for a small fortune.

We crossed the Tigris and headed south towards the hotel. The people were out on the streets and all looked rather shell shocked. They looked as if they were unsure about whether to be happy, relieved or concerned. Most managed to combine all three. Before we knew it we were stuck in a throng of people who looked like they were marching towards the Palestine Hotel. They seemed very interested in us and our Land Rover Discovery. Not the most inconspicuous vehicle to be driving around in, but it was marginally better than a bright yellow van. We drove with the flow of the people, concerned that the good nature of the crowd could change at any moment and indeed the tension seemed to rise as they approached the hotel. The Palestine hotel overlooked the remains of the statue of Saddam that we all saw being pulled down by the Iraqis at the end of the war. The square and the feet of the statue that remained looked much smaller than I imagined. I wondered why they filmed this particular statue, as there were more impressive statues, murals and paintings all over the capital. My questions were answered when I looked up and saw the TV cameras bristling from the sides of the Palestine, sprouting from every balcony and the roof. The world's press, confined to the Palestine, had merely zoomed their cameras in on the nearest statue to them. The hotel, like all the other buildings was architecturally impressive, but had had 12 years of neglect and this was a feeling one had throughout Baghdad. I could see that it must have been a prosperous city and why in the late seventies it was often referred to the Vegas of the Middle East. We edged our way through the crowd, parked up outside the hotel and wandered in to see what was going on in 'the best hotel in Baghdad'.

The foyer was crammed with journalists all frantically jabbering away to each other whilst trying to listen to what the journalist next to them was talking about. They all had their own security guards who mothered over them to ensure they didn't do anything too reckless. Inevitably security often got in the way of a good story but when they did find themselves in a spot of bother they were on hand to extract them to safety. The volumes in the foyer suddenly began to reach a crescendo and the journalists were herded upstairs. To our horror we saw that we were caught in a riot as the demonstrators we had driven through five minutes ago now clambered over each other in an attempt to get into the hotel. A ring of troops was holding them back and it transpired that the crowd was there to get jobs. Someone had been handing out job applications from the hotel the previous day and the news had spread. We were trapped. So we did the obvious thing and sat down to have a drink and savour the atmosphere, whilst trying to look as calm as possible. But there was a small flaw to our plan - the hotel was dry. There was, however, a beer man selling his own version of a strong continental lager on the other side of the crowd. I was concerned that we may be offending the Iraqis by drinking alcohol but I was informed that until relatively recently it was the norm. Indeed our tourist map had shown us there had been a plethora of clubs and bars that lined the Tigris, but as Saddam had aligned himself with the more radical religious leaders they had been closed down. Buying a round of drinks took on a whole new meaning as we were forced to ease our way through the crowd and back again. Fortunately the focus of the Iraqi anger was on the Coalition Forces and they found it fairly amusing to have us squeezing through them with our ill-gotten gains.

A little while later, feeling slightly happier about the situation, we decided to brave it out and return to the airport. It was about an hour and a half before it got dark and we needed to get back to our luxury accommodation. We managed to find our way through the debris strewn-streets of Baghdad and to the Coalition checkpoint barring access to the airport. This is where the fun started. We got out our passports and were told that we couldn't come in because we had no ID. Passports were not good enough, we needed plastic ID. 'Where do we get ID from?' 'You don't' was the response. 'It hasn't been issued yet'. It may sound amusing but we were on the wrong side of the fence and it was getting dark. We went through the various stages of diplomacy; charm, flattery, anger and then skirted around the begging stage. 'Not my problem Sir' was the soldier's final word. There followed an exchange that didn't do much for the 'special' relationship and we did a sharp U-turn whilst trying to look nonchalant and totally in control of the whole situation.

The relaxed front was as much for the soldier's benefit as our own. The jovial atmosphere in the car changed to one of tension as we realised that we were going to have to find somewhere to stay. Even Gavin, our regional head of security who had joined us for a couple of days was looking mildly concerned. It was essential we found somewhere before it got dark. We had been warned in the Palestine Hotel that with darkness came an increase in lawlessness, which often took the form of car jacking and shootings. We were a little worried. However there was a glimmer of hope, as we had seen a map of the airport and knew there was another route in through the north-western side, through Abu Garab, a particularly lawless suburb of Baghdad and home of one of Saddam's more infamous jails. It was a gamble but when we looked at the alternatives it was one worth taking. We headed off back towards town and proceeded to edge our way around the outside of the airport. This was easier said than done as the majority of the roads were blocked with rubble or burned out vehicles. We ended up driving through some very run down areas. There wasn't a great deal of banter going on in the car and the darker it got the more the tension built. Eventually we found an entrance and decided that the policy would be to wave our passports, look as official as possible and not to stop. We drove through the gate, the unsuspecting sentry was asleep and wasn't on his feet until we were but a trail of dust in the night.

Night one in the hangar proved to be more eventful than anticipated. All around the airport we could hear gunfire and explosions, so we turned on our stereo, cracked open the Jack Daniels and had a few night caps to help ease ourselves off to sleep. The soldiers were like moths to a light and a couple of them joined us for a drink. They had been dry for six months so in hindsight plying them with Tennessee's favourite tipple wasn't the brightest thing to do but we did it anyway. As the conversation flowed we became more and more amazed at how naïve these guys were. I had heard the statistic that only 10% of Americans have a passport but never really thought about it until I had met one of the 90%. It then dawned on me how skewed their view of current affairs really is. We were with reservists who had been pulled from their jobs and sent to war for a year. I suppose they should have read the small print and realised that with the way the world is going the chances of them remaining as weekend warriors in the reserves were slim. Nevertheless I did feel sorry for them - a year is a long time to be away from friends and family.

Gavin opened the singing with American Pie and an Elvis number before, as is inevitable with soldiers, the conversation quickly turned to 'poon-tang' as they fondly referred to it. There followed a series of gag inducing stories about their previous sexual conquests. I won't go into all of them but one went a bit like this. You'll have to imagine an inebriated Texan drawling the following 'I was at home in Texas and I met this one girl, in a bar. She wasn't young, in fact she was as old as my Mom, but you know what, just because there is snow on the mountains it doesn't mean there ain't fire down below.' I asked him if he had a family and he explained that he was happily married. He continued 'that reminds me I've told my wife that when I go, I want to be buried in a thong and a pair of flip flops.' 'Why?' I dutifully asked. 'Because it's gonna be hot where I'm going (hell) and I want to be well prepared! So where were we? Ah yes I'd been talkin' to this chick and she was comin' on all hot and I thought yeaaah, here we go. She musta weighed in at bout 150lbs, anywase I managed to get her into the car and drove round to her house. We were on the couch and the lights were off and I was good and ready. I stripped off her top and started sucking her nipple. She began to squeal. She was lovin' it. Suddenly her nipple exploded and warm puss oozed into my mouth. I jumped off the dirty bitch and turned the lights on. She was lying on the couch and I saw that I had been sucking on a boil next to her nipple. Man that was gross.' The story continued but I think you have the gist of the tone. For an hour we listened with morbid fascination as the stories became more fantastic and then we made our excuses and went to bed. But that was not the end of it. Having been asleep for an hour I realized there was someone in the room and I heard a stage whisper right:

'Hey Phil, hey Phil'

'Yes'

'Am gonna go get me some pussy, you want some?'

'No thank you'

'You want some pussy Phil?'

'No thank you, now fuck off.'

'Aw Phil, well I'm gonna go get me some'

I went to sleep shaking my head in disbelief. Twenty four hours earlier I had been having dinner in the Ivy and now there I was in Saddam International Airport on a camp bed in a hangar. As I reflected on the day and thought about what I had left behind, I began to wonder whether I had bitten off more than I could chew. The more conservative side of me was chastising my adventurous side for accepting such a ridiculous job. I went to sleep with my mind in turmoil. And we never did hear if the soldier found true love that night.

The following morning my thoughts returned to those of the night before. Mentally I pulled myself together and realised that thoughts like these were going to have a negative affect. I gave myself a lecture, the core themes of which were 'you've made your bed, so you will have to lie in it' and 'you've got your new challenge, so rise to it'. The first challenge of the day was to find some washing facilities. After much searching we realized that bottles of Evian were the only option. We couldn't continue like this forever so we found an old freight container, a barrel, a pick and chopped the end off a fire hose. It was Blue Peter all over again. We made another hole in the bottom of the barrel and put the hose into this then made a hole in the top of the container. We threaded the hose through the container roof and filled the barrel with water ensuring that the hose was in the closed position. If you are ever in this situation, remember to make a hole in the bottom of the container so the water will drain away and if possible get a wooden pallet to stand on. Hey presto a shower and it only took a whole morning to build! Having made life a little more bearable it was time to get down to business.

4 FIRST MOVER ADVANTAGE

There is no point having first mover advantage if you do not have a strategy to stay there. First and foremost, you need to understand the competition. You need to be prepared to act immediately and ruthlessly to protect your position. And you need to make sure you are firmly embedded in the local market and constantly apprised of developments.

(The Encyclopedia of Current Business Orthodoxy)

Our remit was fairly clear; we had been told that the target for the first year was a $2m profit. It was time to make the most of being first into Iraq. So that afternoon we went straight to the core of potential business and gained access to the Mayor's meeting. We introduced ourselves to the Mayor of the airport, a military Colonel, cigar clamped between his teeth. The meeting was filled with representatives from all the units based at the airport and the newest addition, DHL. We did a pitch to them and were met with silence, of the stunned variety. But after the initial shock there was an outbreak of whooping and hollering as they realised they could now get kit and equipment and any other home comforts they wanted sent out to them. Not one of my more difficult sells. The problem was going to be delivering on the pitch. The important thing, however, was that we had gained the attention of the guys who controlled 15,000 troops at the airport. We deftly fielded questions about flight regularity because we didn't even know when the next plane would be coming in and pledged to come round and see them all to set up the accounts. Now we needed to make sure we remained there and engrained ourselves in all aspects of their logistics process before any of the competition came to the party. The Mayor, having had the wind taken out of his sails, continued his conference. With a flourish of his cigar he mentioned that the first delivery of the portaloos they had ordered from Kuwait had finally arrived. This was obviously his piece de resistance but by this stage, the rest of the meeting were dreaming of the pretzels and cheese dips they were going to have sent over from home. The Colonel's last ten minutes were then hijacked by the Padre who said some prayers, gave a brief sermon and demanded to know why various units had not been coming to church. Heads were hung in shame, excuses were mumbled, and consignments of beef jerky and potato chips were ordered from the US. We left the meeting and went to explore the airport and work out where the thirty five units were actually located.

However before we started our tour - and whilst we were in their good books - we requested and acquired enough rations to feed us for a week and then sorted out our pass situation before our next foray into Baghdad. The airport is much like any other international airport except that it was built from scratch and did not have to grow piece by piece, fighting for space as it did so. Saddam simply allocated some land and built it. As a result it occupies a huge area. It has a couple of runways and three main terminals. On the eastern side of the airport was a fourth terminal, a special terminal, set back amongst the trees. It contained it's own hospital, a helipad and some luxury accommodation. This had been built for Saddam but must have rarely been used - certainly his international air miles account hadn't reached redeemable status. It would have been for internal flights only but he was paranoid about the planes being sabotaged by foreign agencies and therefore this prevented him flying at all. Ironically, it was now occupied by the CIA. We wandered through the main terminals. Debris lay strewn about the floor. Water had flooded the building and the doors had suffered a similar fate to those in our accommodation. Furthermore every pane of glass had a crack or bullet hole in it. Blatant destruction is what sprang to mind and it wasn't long before soldiers were put on guard to prevent people having a look or taking photos. They feared the press more than anyone as it was clear that most of the damage had been done after the airport was captured.

At the north western end of the terminals was a rather forlorn group of Iraqi Airways planes. The Iraqis had removed their engines prior to the war. The idea was to prevent the planes being mistaken for aircraft that could be used against the Coalition. It had indeed prevented them being bombed but hadn't stopped them being used as target practice by the troops. As it turned out the Iraqis had inadvertently written the planes off themselves. For future reference you should bear in mind that if you are removing engines from the wings of your plane you should replace them with a similar weight. If you don't, the wings will rise and the body and structure of the plane will become contorted rendering it useless. I had seen enough and we headed off to try and acquire a piece of paper that was going to get us back into the airport. We were given various names and were assured that these would smooth our next attempt at re-entry.

Back in Baghdad the city was buzzing. I couldn't help getting the rather false impression that Baghdad was thriving. This was because the people themselves are well educated and incredibly warm and welcoming, particularly with the British. I found this slightly surprising after the way in which we had treated them in the past. But having spoken to the Iraqis they were eternally grateful for the administrative system that the British put in place, particularly on the education and health services front. I suspect this is because education is the one thing they had clung onto as it represented an exit to the western world. It also meant that if they were ever free of Saddam they would be able to survive on the world stage. On our return to the Palestine we noticed a competitor had set up a desk in the foyer. I did some detective work and found out that they were actually acting as agents and were therefore probably doing it illegally. My next stop was to have a meeting with the General Manager of the hotel to see how we could rectify the situation. We were ushered into Osama's office. He hastily told us he was no relation to Bin Laden and talked us through the procedure to get the competition ousted from the foyer. It was clear that it was going to involve some brown envelopes and then a monthly fee to ensure the prime spot and their swift removal. Envelopes were duly handed over to the relevant people and the deal was sealed with a cup of strong coffee and a handshake. We were pleased to report to our network that DHL were going to open their first office two weeks after the end of the war. It was referred to as an 'Express Centre' which is a rather grand term for a desk but it was a start and our first foray into business in Iraq.

The launch party for the opening of our Express Centre

attracted some thirsty journalists although not quite the hoards we were expecting. But the word soon spread and before long the desk was attracting considerable attention. There was, however, an immediate dilemma in the form of EU sanctions, which put us in the awkward position of not being able to begin commercial activity. So to the frustration of our customers we spent our time promoting the service to come. The development of commercial business was always going to be slow and secondary. Really we were relying on the trade of the businesses that came in on the back of the USAID contracts as these were going to be the basis for success in the short term. Local commercial business was always going to be a longer-term goal - not least because local industries had been decimated during the UN sanctions. Now they were relying on the injection of US cash to kick-start the economy. The problem was that at this stage the basic infrastructure did not exist to support large corporations. Intermittent electricity and water and no communications other than satellite phones meant that even the minimum expectations of a western company were not being met. These factors, combined with the unstable security situation, merely increased the barriers for entry to foreign companies. However it was already clear that those that grasped the nettle, like DHL, were clearly going to reap the rewards.

Loitering around the foyer of the Palestine one day we began chatting to a young Iraqi called Ziad. He spoke better English than our Arabic, so we asked him to act as our guide and went for a drive around the city. It was a sweltering hot day and Baghdad like any other large city suffers from traffic jams. We made a sluggish journey around town and asked to be taken to the German and British Embassies as we wanted to pitch to both and also register with the latter. Ziad obviously had his own agenda and must have been under strict instructions because before we knew it we were drinking tea with his father, Ahmed. We spent a long time chatting about the war, their hopes and fears and a little about Saddam. They were reticent when it came to the latter, still unable to mention his name without looking around them and dropping their voice - such was the fear with which he was held.

We asked about their lives during the war and what it was like being in Baghdad. It seemed that many of the people of Baghdad left the city and stayed with relatives during the war, particularly the wives and the children. Often the men stayed behind to protect their houses from the looters. Now that people were beginning to filter back, the lawlessness was their biggest fear. We were keen to rectify our dismal accommodation and Ahmed promised to sort us out with a house or at least someone who knew someone who would sort us out with a house. There was obviously going to be a finder's fee but we were told not to worry about this as he was going to get it from the person whose house we let. That didn't sound like an ideal way of doing business so I suggested that I would do a little market research. This involved a couple of calls to people we had met in the Palestine to get a rough price for houses. Having been shown a property I then suggested a price to Ahmed and told him he would get his fee for haggling the seller down to this and 25% of anything below it. This seemed to work quite well and before we knew it we had several six bedroom properties to lease for $30,000 a year. I was surprised at how property prices had held their value and disturbed at how quickly they were rising. The main reason for this was the UN and the Red Cross, who were willing to pay whatever they were asked. A house we would pay $30,000 for, they would pay $90,000 resulting in a rapidly over inflated market. Ziad's family turned out to be a well-known middle class family who had their own engineering business before the war. We subsequently employed Ziad, the eldest son and a couple of his friends to man the desk at the Palestine.

5 BUILDING BUSINESS PROCESS

Once established, an operation should focus on building business process to ensure maximum efficiency and effectiveness. Process is the platform that enables a firm to provide their customers with reliable expectations as well as the security and predictability that helps offset the inevitable uncertainties.

(The Encyclopedia of Current Business Orthodoxy)

Try working in an environment without email or telephones, not just devoid of mobiles but landlines as well. I had all sorts of great ideas of establishing a business process and ensuring efficiency but in reality, despite it being 2003, we had returned to business as it must have been done 40 years ago. We did have satellite phones but these only worked outside. So unless I was standing outside I was unable to receive a call, rendering them next to useless. It meant we had to adapt rapidly and we worked out two basic processes for arranging meetings. Option one was to drive to an office/house and hope that the prospective attendees were there. This only had a 20% success rate, particularly as unannounced visitors were largely ignored. Option two involved telling Ziad who we needed to see. At the end of the day he headed off to knock on doors and try and find out when people were available. That night he would confirm a time slot with them and then give us the details the following morning in time to get there ourselves. Having just come from London, without thinking, I initially tried for four meetings in a day. This was totally unrealistic as it did not allow for road blocks, punctures and a lot of sitting around waiting and chatting. A much more realistic figure was one a day, perhaps two at a stretch. At least it had the positive effect of teaching us to be sure that we did not forget to thoroughly discuss everything on the agenda. There was no question of being able to fire off an email afterwards to clarify a point raised during the meeting. Ziad soon helped us find a house we liked and we then had a most amusing conversation with the owner who lived off High St Kensington in London. She had left the property fifteen years earlier and was keen to hear how it had fared. Structurally it was sound but it had been gutted. Having negotiated our price we were to learn later that afternoon that the hierarchy in Bahrain did not want us to have a villa; they felt we were moving too quickly! Actually speed was essential as housing prices were doubling on a weekly basis, but they would not be swayed.

We eventually managed to get to the embassies but a couple of days later than anticipated. We went to see the British first of all as it seemed that everyone in Baghdad knew where this was. The caretaker who had been looking after the embassy for the past 12 years had been replaced by a platoon of Paratroopers who now manned the gate and guarded the complex. We were ushered in and went to see the Head of Mission who was busy organising portacabins on the lawn in front of the embassy building. We persuaded him to have a break and sat him down to talk about what we could do for him and also to let him know that we were British passport holders. We should have guessed that the fact that he was in a similar position to everyone else and was trying to organise somewhere to stay meant that our presence in Baghdad was not going to be greeted with a fanfare or even a raised eyebrow. We went for a walk around the old embassy building which was now inhabited by the paratroopers, who had convinced the staff that there was a health and safety issue which resulted in the building being condemned and them having a roof over their heads. We also learnt that the caretaker had done such a fantastic job looking after the place that everything had remained untouched. There was one member of the staff who had been there 12 years earlier and was the first back into the embassy after the war. On walking into his old office there were cups of tea, cigarettes in ashtrays, newspapers and all the usual office paraphernalia exactly as it had been left. The only change was the yellowing paper and dusty surfaces. The paratroopers had their priorities and the pool had been refilled and a game of water polo was going on.

We then moved onto the German embassy which was a different scene altogether. We met the First Secretary who was trying to rescue what little furniture remained and was beside himself with despair at the discovery that the building had been gutted. He started to rant about the US soldiers he had seen on the news, watching the Iraqis loot the embassy and asked me why they had not done anything to stop it happening. As a diplomat I would have thought that it was clear to him that the German's pre war stance on Iraq had hardly endeared themselves to the Coalition Forces, but I felt it was not the time to point this out to him. Also, this was not a moment to set out our stall and so we offered our condolences and drove off to find the Australian Embassy and look for a warehouse.

It was whilst we were driving around Baghdad looking for offices and a warehouse that we had our first incident. The Iraqis tended to drive very slowly, for a variety of reasons, not least because their cars were often held together by string. I had decided that as we stuck out like a sore thumb we should drive quickly, particularly down the motorways where there tend to be more incidents. That afternoon, we were heading up a flyover when some shots rang out over my right shoulder and we turned round to see the Iraqi driver behind us slew to one side of the road. It was evident that we were an opportune target but had been travelling a little too quickly for our aggressors who had completely under estimated our speed and shot the car behind us. It was clear that the security situation was going to drive our business development and I managed to get an official update, from the military, sent through the following day.

SECURITY BRIEF: 01 May 2003

Travel in Iraq entails risk
- Variety of armed gunmen remain at large.
  - Criminal elements
  - Regime elements
  - Foreign Influences

- Vehicle accidents are a serious concern.

Hostile Activity
- Convoy ambushed along highway ten near FALLUJAH.

- Rocket Propelled Grenades (RPGs) / small arms fired. Two civilian truck drivers wounded.

- Patrol attacked at AL MAQDIDIYAH (NE of BAQUBAH).
  - RPGs /small arms fired. Nine captured.

- Protesters threw grenades at soldiers in downtown HIT.
  - Crowd angry about U.S. detaining three suspects.
  - Three soldiers wounded, two civilians wounded.

- Convoy attacked 42 km North of BAGHDAD.
  - Small arms fired. One soldier killed.
  - Location: 38SMC291220 33 38 08N 044 14 08E.

- Patrol hit landmine hidden under a sandbag 25 km SW BAGHDAD.
  - Flare fired before attack. Two soldiers wounded.
  - Location: 38SMB288538 33 01 13N 044 14 16E.

Coalition Security Activity

- 4th Infantry Division conducted a cordon and search operation near BAYJI that resulted in the capture of two key area Fedayeen leaders. Soldiers also detained ten former regime Special Security Organization agents and several former regime senior military officers for questioning.

- 3rd Armored Cavalry Regiment raided the residence that they believed belongs to the ringleader of a group responsible for attacks on Coalition convoys on Highway ten. He and an Iraqi male were captured along with numerous weapons.

- Marines from 3rd Battalion, 7th Marine Regiment, along with Civil Affairs, Governance Support Teams and military police recently conducted a sweep of the KARBALA city market to combat illegal arms sales. They arrested four Iraqis and confiscated several AK-47 rifles.

- 2nd Brigade Combat Team searched and found a cache of weapons, explosives and communications equipment near a radio and TV station in MOSUL. The cache included an anti-aircraft gun, 40 rocket-propelled grenade launchers, two AK-47 rifles, encrypted radio systems and a large amount of ammunition and rockets.

Police Activity in the Last 24 Hours:
CENTCOM Press Release: 03-05-104

- A local schoolteacher recently showed a joint patrol of Iraqi police and 549th Military Police some landmines other citizens had found in a BAGHDAD neighborhood.

- A shooter on a rooftop recently fired at members of the 233rd Military Police Company while they were on patrol in BAGHDAD. The patrol withheld their fire because they could not positively identify the shooter's position.

- 233rd Military Police soldiers and Iraqi police, on a joint patrol in BAGHDAD, saw four men attempting to forcefully enter a house. The men fled, dropping an AK-47 rifle, when the patrol approached. The patrol searched the area for the men, but could not find them.

As you can see from the report, the Coalition had not quite won the war and were beginning to have difficulties controlling Baghdad. It was no small task but I felt the soldiers were being rather heavy handed and aggressive. This was really due to a lack of experience on their part and also due to a total lack of understanding of the culture within which they found themselves. For example it was incredibly demeaning for a male Iraqi to have a female soldier stop him and get him out of his car at gunpoint. They also had the wrong type of troops in Baghdad. They were not used to patrolling on foot and winning the battle for hearts and minds. As a result they had a radically different approach to winning the peace than the British troops. When on patrol, the British tended to do it on foot, in Baghdad the troops drove around in armoured cars that bristled with machine guns. The US forces had achieved a stunning victory in the war and that is what they are very good at; but their whole mentality is geared towards things happening quickly. Whether ordering a burger or winning the peace, they expected a wholehearted adaptation of US principles and a swift acceptance of a Western type of democracy. If only life was that easy. The British took a far more pragmatic approach and their experience in Northern Ireland, where they had been trying to win the peace for over 25 years, really became apparent.

Despite the criticism, I can't come up with an easy solution, it is going to take a long time and I think that this is an aspect that the Coalition did not really think about. It seems that they only really had one goal; to oust Saddam in the belief that everything would then fall into place. The difficulty the troops faced was exacerbated by a criminal element who were exploiting the instability. This resulted in random shootings and car-jackings and ultimately led to the

Coalition Forces imposing a curfew from 11-6, something that should have really been imposed from day one. Furthermore it was clear that if ORHA (Office of Reconstruction and Humanitarian Assistance) didn't sort the infrastructure out quickly civil unrest would develop and spread. Compounding the problem in post war Iraq was unemployment which was rampant as 70% of the population had been employed by the state. I began to hear some Iraqis express the belief that although he was no good, at least the people had jobs, electricity, food and water under Saddam.

6 INVESTING IN PRODUCTIVITY

The right equipment is essential in any situation. Botched tools will result in a botched job. They also create a psychology of 'inadequacy' rather than 'excellence'. Settling for being content just to get by will breed mediocrity rather than a determination to be the best.

(The Encyclopedia of Current Business Orthodoxy)

Our communications continued to be an utter nightmare. We had been struggling to get any information back to Bahrain. Whilst at the airport, the satellite phones only worked when I was standing outside in the middle of the runway, the tarmac melting around my feet. Twice a day, we would launch a two man operation to attempt to get the email working. One of us would sit in the car with the air condition on full blast. The other was in the hot seat, outside, speaking to an IT 'expert' in Dubai whilst shouting instructions through a gap in the car window. We would then move our little satellite dish this way and that, changing its angle, praising it, stroking it and cursing it but to no avail. It got to the point where we called people in the UK to access our email accounts and read through our emails over the satellite phone and respond accordingly. A number of the so called experts were sent out to try and rectify the problem but with little luck. Eventually someone who knew what they were doing turned up. It was thanks to the arrival of an IT guru from Dubai, who took the form of an Indian called Milan, that we managed to get our email satellite link up and running. We repeated our tried and tested format and I sat in the Land Rover with the air condition on, in front of the aircraft hangar, trying to keep cool in 50 degrees heat. The small satellite dish was sitting in front of the car and was visibly sinking into the tarmac. Milan was under pressure. He was desperate not to miss the flight home as the last time he had come out to fix a problem was in Afghanistan and he ended up having to stay overnight. He had stayed just down the road from The American Embassy where a massive bomb had gone off and he could clearly envisage the same happening out here. I tried to convince him that all was safe but he looked at me as if I was mad and, as if on cue, the gunfire crackled in the background. He didn't believe it was the Americans practicing on the firing range.

At last his persistence came to fruition and he fixed the problem. I joked that he would be back on the next flight as no doubt it was a temporary fix. He wasn't listening and began to sprint across the runway to the plane. As he was rushing away I heard a clunk, clunk behind me. I turned around to see that an American GI had managed to drive over the satellite in his Hum V (like a Land Rover but bigger) putting us back to square one. There followed a fairly frank conversation about the individual's awareness made worse by his attempts to mollify two very irate red-faced Englishmen by saying he would fix my $4000 satellite with his Swiss army penknife. I left Phil contemplating a variety of painful scenarios for the GI and went over and hauled poor old Milan out of the plane. We persuaded him that he should come and stay at the Palestine Hotel, which didn't elicit much enthusiasm. We had been kicked out of our room on the first floor of the hangar when it was pointed out that 20 soldiers would be occupying the space two of us were in. So, camp beds under our arms and bags on our backs, we had gone in search of a new corner. We had cleverly discovered a small windowless room with air conditioning which drew a lot of envious looks and resulted in just a little gloating on our behalf. Predictably though, like children with a new toy, the first night we cranked the aircon up to the maximum. Our theory had been to freeze the mosquitos to death but part of the way through the night the machine shuddered to a halt and our windowless box room turned into a mosquito infested sauna. According to our thermometer it was 110 degrees. I was visibly shrinking and had begun to look like a prune. There was no way we could fit another body in there. So we took the now familiar trip into town and arrived in the hotel with our pieces of satellite and left Milan in his room trying to fix it.

Later that evening I called Milan on the phone. He asked me to wait a moment and I could hear him answering the bell boy's knock at the door. We continued talking but I could sense he was distracted. Then I heard him saying 'stop this, no hanky panky, my friend' and asked him what he was up to. He explained that he had taken his shirt off earlier because of the heat. Having returned to the phone after answering the door, the bell boy had stalked him across the room and started stroking the hair on his chest whilst he was talking to me on the phone. He was not impressed. (Unfortunately for us, the Hotel and its staff were frequently up to no good. It had a captive audience and so it could act as it pleased. At $120 a night you found yourself in a retro seventies room with worn out carpets and a shower that didn't work.) The rest of the night was spent mollifying a disgruntled Milan and telling him about our latest soldier stories.

The subject of soldiers' sex had come up again the previous day and they had told us that some female soldiers, on a base in the North of Iraq, had been sent home for lewd behaviour. It turned out that they had been selling condoms. The asking price was a massive fifty dollars, but intercourse was thrown in for free. That was how they got around the prostitution clause of their contract. The 'loving' couples found their privacy by climbing onto the roof of the hangar at the airport. They were making a small fortune. It briefly occurred to us that perhaps we should set up a brothel - there was clearly no shortage of demand. But a more sober state of the mind the next morning drew us back to our senses, not least when we tried to think of how we might explain our entrepreneurial thinking to family back home.

ORHA was headed by Jay Garner and was the new governing body of Iraq. It was housed in an area in the crook of the Tigris. The area consisted of about ten palaces that had been occupied by Saddam and his sons. It had an inner cordon where they had lived and an outer cordon that housed various parts of the Republican Guard and Saddam's retinue. The palaces were vast and sprawling, with every immediate facility, including hospitals in the basement in bunkers and more gold furniture than you can shake a stick at. The primary ambition of their designers had clearly been exhibitionism because for all the marble the rest of the fabric was cheap. The furniture looked lavish and expensive but was made of plywood and given a quick coat of gold paint. The main Palace had four huge busts of Saddam gazing down imperiously from the roof. They looked bronze but were really fiberglass and their flimsiness merely reinforced my view that the whole regime was propped up by a thin façade of fear built around his image. Inside, there were hundreds of rooms and I wondered if he ever even went upstairs. In his absence, the corridors were littered with GIs who lay, gently sweating, in the corners and under the windows desperate to get out of the heat. At the eastern end of the palace, there was a room with one-way mirrors that overlooked a huge ballroom. This was where Uday used to pick his virgins from a naked parade below. As I walked through the corridors I began to understand why this man had to be removed and though I was unsure of the reasons given for the war I began to grasp the enormity of what he did to the country and its people.

Outside, a huge swimming pool was being slowly filled and even half full it provided the soldiers a moments respite from the searing heat. There were several high diving boards and I pictured Saddam doing a huge belly flop in his Speedos in front of a sycophantic crowd. Parked near the front gate was a coach with blacked out windows. This was where the cabinet would meet and then be driven off to a secret destination before sitting with Saddam. Prior to the meetings they would be checked through a number of x-ray machines. All they were allowed into the meeting was the clothes they wore, such was his paranoia. I'm told that there was an occasion at one of the last cabinet meetings when the Minister for Justice took a quick look at his watch. Saddam noticed and at the end of the meeting he made the minister stay in his chair for 48 hours before returning to put a bullet through his head. His lack of trust enveloped all aspects of his life. He used to drive in a convoy of ten black Mercedes with darkened windows. None of the drivers knew if he was in their car and the cars would be constantly changing their position in the convoy. Then, every 10km all the drivers would be changed so that they never knew where he had come from or where he was going. I met a man who was a chef in the palace who said that all the 52 palaces had to cook 40 meals each day in the expectation that he would be there. In reality he rarely went to a palace, often staying at people's houses. Meanwhile his population was starving and the food had to be thrown away. Anyone found eating the food would face unmentionable reprisals. It was clear that the UN sanctions had failed. They had helped destroy Iraq whilst Saddam embezzled what little money came into the country, leaving the population too weak to do anything about it. The reasons given for going to war may well be a discussion point for years to come, but from what I had seen, the man was a monster who dominated a population who were not going to be able to oust him without foreign intervention.

7 MARKETING

Projecting a consistent identity to existing and potential customers is vital to enduring success. A product needs to be liked and this can be achieved by pursuing familiarity and developing a relationship that feels almost personal with its market. Never assume superiority or the certainty of customer affection.

(The Encyclopedia of Current Business Orthodoxy)

ORHA gave daily briefings to Non Governmental Organisations (NGOs) such as charities and we went to a couple of these in the first few weeks. The idea was that the administration briefed the agencies on the safe and unsafe areas, the latest security incidents and gave feedback on the regions they felt were in the greatest need of aid. The problem was these meetings tended to be hijacked by a small group of NGOs that were more pious than the others and the meetings developed into a theoretical debate. The usual issue was one of semantics revolving around whether the army Colonel who had given the brief was using the correct language to describe the types of aid. It was totally unreasonable behaviour - here were the US attempting to ease the lives of the aid agencies and they were getting bogged down in a mire of triviality. It was a problem that consumed them in all aspects of their work in Iraq. I quickly realised that we were wasting our time with the aid agencies so took some direct action. At the end of the meeting we went and asked the Colonel if there was anything that was of vital importance that we could help with. He mentioned that there was an orphanage that needed gas to cook food and sterilise equipment. So, for a meagre $200 we were able to ensure a temporary respite for a few months. We mentioned this to head office who decided that DHL would donate 25 tonnes of aid to five of the worst orphanages. This put some NGO noses out of joint but it was certainly the most direct way we could think of helping a little and supported the marketing line that we were there to help rebuild the country.

We met up with the Civil Affairs unit of the army and spent the next few days wandering through hospitals and orphanages. The Civil Affairs unit, a good example of the Coalition thinking ahead, was designed to liaise with the civil population and then guide the military towards the best way of helping the needy. Unfortunately they were woefully undermanned and faced with a major city suffering from infrastructural meltdown. Nevertheless they kindly spared a soldier to take us around the orphanages. I'm squeamish at the best of times and was satisfied to believe that the conditions were awful. I therefore asked to talk to the administrators so that we could get an idea of the type of equipment that they most needed. Sure enough, the first place we went into I was taken through the children's ward. I did not need to be a doctor to understand that basic medical supplies were lacking and we were shown some horrific injuries and illnesses that had been caused by a combination of Saddam, UN sanctions and Allied bombing.

On the business front I delivered my first DHL letter to

Mr. Bremer, who had taken over from Garner in mid May. He oozed an air of efficiency, was clearly keen to get things moving and was interested to hear about DHL's initiative in Iraq. I must say being a postman is slightly overrated, particularly in the context of the previous day's delivery of 25 tonnes of aid to five orphanages around the city. The aid, which sounded like a terrific idea at the time, had arrived in the middle of the day and the two of us had unloaded it by hand from the Antonov. Then we stacked it onto pallets. It ranged from bleach to footballs and nappies. Whilst I was clutching a box of nappies I heard a peal of laughter behind me and turned round to see Mark, an old friend, who had just arrived in Iraq to work for a security company. Having spun a yarn about how important I was having left the city to set up DHL in Iraq, he was amused to see me lugging boxes of nappies from one end of a warehouse to another.

The following morning, Phil and I, watched by a platoon of soldiers, loaded 25 tonnes of rice, bleach, tins of food, toys, dettol, nappies, footballs and water into the trucks. By the time we arrived at the first orphanage we were nicely warmed up. The orphanages themselves were for children aged from 3 to 17. At the first I chatted to a group of 12 children that had been picked up a fortnight ago, having spent four weeks living on a roundabout. The second orphanage catered for orphans with mental disorders and they were a terrific help in unloading, even if some of the goods got carried in slightly the wrong direction. They were obviously starved of any stimulation and so were itching to get involved. It was touching to see children in wheelchairs moving boxes from the trucks into the storeroom. By the time we had unloaded the third truck I can safely say I had been truly fried by the sun and was glad to have an hour in the aircon of the car as we sat in a traffic jam on our way to the next destination.

Like any other city in the world there are huge traffic jams throughout the day. But unlike many cities there was a distinct lack of any kind of highway code. If you needed to get somewhere, roads, lanes, pavements and direction of traffic were ignored. At night it became particularly hazardous as many of the cars did not have lights and none of the streets were lit. I found the best thing to do was to drive with the windows open and listen for the rattle of an approaching car as this would often herald their arrival long before they were picked out by my headlights. Obviously you could only do this if your car was rattle free and so around town there were frequent crashes. Fortunately everyone was usually travelling so slowly that there were no serious injuries. The standard of vehicles being driven around was gradually improving as people dusted off cars that had been hidden in garages and imports from the Far East, via Jordan began to flood the market.

We arrived at our final orphanage and offloaded the last of the supplies. There was no avoiding the inevitable exhaustion and we ended the day on our knees. Re-hydration was a priority but despite this, a combination of the sun and 'gifts' we had eaten at the various orphanages led to a serious bout of Baghdad belly. It is never convenient to get a dodgy belly but this was possibly the most inconvenient. The loos were about 200m away from our hangar room and unlit because there was still no electricity. Although Imodium and various blockers are good there are some strains that they really can't cope with. Cleverly, I had managed to find one of those strains. After some days of gut wrenching stomach churning followed by a sprint to the latrines, I resorted to starvation. Never one to willingly miss a meal, this was the last option. But in Iraq it was not that difficult, as the Iraqi diet was limited due to the lack of food and I had thrown my last ration pack to a child on the motorway. Naively I thought these were going to be eaten by them. However in hindsight a bottle of tabasco, chicken pasta and some peanut butter and crackers would have probably put them into the state I was in. A few days later we were walking through a market and I noticed ration packs for sale for $3 a packet. More disturbing was the sight of Food Aid and sacks of UN rice that were also being sold in abundance.

Our commercial business was still on ice but the military business, in pleasing contrast, was destined to go through the roof. Following the rapturous support at the Mayor's meeting, we decided to drive around the country and visit various military bases, targeting those with 15000 or more troops. The idea was that these could then become international gateways for aircraft and could form part of the hub and spoke system that would stretch throughout the country. In the short term the key was to get an ex-pat onto each base to provide and sell the service. This was essential as the bases offered security for the employee and a captive audience of 15000 troops. Whilst this was going on, the US mail contract was sealed and we also began to win the accounts for priority parts. A priority part could be anything from a valve to a helicopter blade. Why didn't they get them through the army system? They could, but it took at least a month compared to two or three days door to door with DHL.

Our first trip was to Balad, in the centre of what became known to the world as the Sunni Triangle. Balad is about an hour's drive north of Baghdad and so we went up to try and find the camp. We knew it was north and stopped to ask for directions on the way there. Ziad was doing the talking but from the body language of those he was questioning I could tell they were not keen to let us know where the military base was. This was obviously an area that staunchly supported Saddam to the extent that one of the sets of directions led us down completely the wrong road. Following our arrival in Balad we went straight to the finance office and began our well rehearsed pitch. The lack of DHL footprint in the US (since rectified following recent acquisitions) meant they hadn't heard of us. We began to explain what we could do for them and why they should open an account. They could not grasp the concept and it was not until we said we provide a similar service to Fedex that we got an 'I understand, why didn't you say that in the first place!' Fedex would have been pleased as punch but as it took them another four months to get to Iraq I know they found the roles had reversed and business acquisition was therefore a little more testing. When we returned to Baghdad International Airport (the Saddam has been dropped) we met the forlorn faces of some other civilian contractors. They informed us of the death of one of their company drivers who transported US Army goods around the country. Every day they had a military escort up to Balad and each day they stopped at the side of the road to pick up some soft drinks. A pattern had been set and that morning they did the same again. As the lead vehicle drove out of the lay-by it depressed an anti tank mine that had been pre-positioned there the previous night. The driver was killed immediately. That night I sat down to write an assessment of the situation in Iraq as I felt it was going to really drive our operation more than the Bahrain Management realised. I wrote the following:

SECURITY BRIEF FOR IRAQ: 19 May 2003

- **General Synopsis**

Following the rampage of looters after the liberation of Baghdad the situation has stabilised to a degree. There remain sporadic outbursts of violence against both Westerners and Iraqis.

- **By Region**

Basra: This town in the south is under the control of the British where they have begun to win the battle for hearts and minds resulting in a degree of normality returning to the area.

Baghdad: In stark contrast to Basra the Coalition Forces are having difficulty maintaining law and order. As the focal point for the country, with the largest concentration of population and wealth, it has understandably become a magnet for the rogue elements operating in Iraq. It is the wealth and the perception of easy pickings that attracts the criminal elements, a problem that is compounded by the fact that no one has a job and people are desperate. There are daily deaths through shootings but there does not seem to be a particular type of target and this adds to the uncertainty. It is assessed that these random shootings may be part of a more concerted attempt to destabilise the situation for the occupying forces. The lack of a judicial system also exacerbates the problem as people realise that they can commit a crime and may be detained for a week but will then be released.

Balad: This military airfield, about two hours drive from Baghdad, is not an urban environment but has still been suffering from daily sniper attacks and when DHL drove up there last week we saw armed civilians at the side of the road.

• **Incident Report**

On Saturday two Iraqi women were dragged from their car, about 150m up the road from the Palestine Hotel, and were both shot dead and then their car was stolen.

A Soldier and a woman were killed at a checkpoint in Baghdad as a result of a drive by shooting.

The DHL staff were threatened at the Express Centre in the Palestine Hotel.

• **Conclusion**

The Express centre will continue to be manned as it is assessed that if DHL closed shop every time there was a threat the business would not get off the ground. Those manning the desk will be briefed on combat indicators that could be a precursor to an attack such as Arabs not being in the reception area (it is usually full of them) and if these occur they should leave the desk until they deem the situation has returned to the normal routine.

It is assessed that with the correct precautions and personal diligence, the employees in Iraq can reduce the risk of exposure to dangerous/life threatening situations. The environment is far from benign but with these steps in place business practices should be able to continue with only minor interruptions.

8 RECRUITMENT

Building a sustainable business is achieved first and foremost by employing the right people. They are the building blocks of trust, efficiency and productivity and these are the prerequisites of longevity.

(The Encyclopedia of Current Business Orthodoxy)

Before long we had employed a couple of adventurous New Zealanders. The first one out had the pleasure of DHL airways care of my Bulgarian friends. He looked suitably shocked when he climbed off the Antonov and explained that the stress of the flight had been enhanced when the Bulgarians stripped off to their grubby Y fronts and the hairiest gave him a wink before settling down to smoke his 20 cigarettes. John made sure his back was to the wall and stayed awake all the way out to Baghdad, this is in spite of it being a 3am flight. I confess that I had 'forgotten' to explain that they always do this because they liked to keep their uniforms clean and because it was so hot on the plane. Meanwhile another of their daring escapades in Afghanistan had also come to light although this time it wasn't really their fault. The plane was parked and General Tommy Franks was visiting the US troops at Bagram airfield. Whilst his Black Hawk helicopter was parking, its blades sliced a hole in the tail of the Antonov.

Phil's first thought was that he would have five unwanted Bulgarians in his tent for the next few days but the Bulgarians, notoriously keen on getting home, had other ideas. Milo promptly climbed up inside the tail and started kicking it back into shape. He then produced four strips of masking tape, uttered a 'no problem' and took off with half the US military, chasing him down the runway. I was just drying my eyes with laughter when I noticed our Antonov taxiing down the runway to prepare for take off. Sure enough there was a member of the US air force chasing them. The crew had forgotten to take the ladder off the side of the plane! As the plane bounced along the runway, the ladder fell off, the US bloke picked it up and continued running after the plane. The pilot must have sensed something was up as he opened his window and stuck his head out of the cockpit. The plane slowed down marginally, the door opened, a hand shot out, a 'no problem' was muttered and on they continued, leaving a rather exasperated US airman looking for myself and Phil as we made ourselves scarce.

My relationship with the coalition was one thing but after three months I received my first kiss from an Iraqi and I realized that my bond with the Iraqis had turned the corner. I should probably qualify that the kiss was from Mohammed, the large bearded man who sold me our beer. I lent my phone to him so that he could call his relatives in Holland. Tears followed and I dodged a bear hug and more kisses whilst trying to haggle over the price of his fake Amstel. I liked to think that I was oiling the wheels of commerce but even without my help life had begun to return to a semblance of normality. For a start I was no longer accosted by people trying to sell me pieces of motorway barrier or snakes from Baghdad Zoo. It appeared that the looting had died down and any that still occurred could be looked upon as finishing a job well done or simply tidying up. The Iraqis had started cleaning their shop fronts, opening them up and getting back to work. Also a large contract had been awarded to tidy up the three months of rubbish, debris and tank hulks that littered the streets and surrounding areas. The bits of shrapnel and piles of burning rubbish that dotted the roads were diminishing daily. This meant that the Ferrari Formula One tyre changers no longer needed to fear for their jobs. The debris that had littered the streets had caused us at least one flat a day which resulted in the DHL tyre changing drills becoming remarkably slick. The fact that people had gone back to work had in turn helped ease the petrol queues, from two days to three hours. This was because many of those who were queuing were simply doing it because they had no job. Having refilled they would then siphon the petrol out of their cars to sell at the side of the road whilst another family member rejoined the line. The schools and Universities had also re-opened but were not fully attended with people remaining wary of the unsettled security situation. In fact we continued to see an interesting pyrotechnic display in Baghdad each night. The Coalition Forces were trying to patrol the streets to quash the crime and this they were doing with varying degrees of competence. Evidently it was thirsty work as I would often see them ambling along carrying crates of Pepsi, having discovered that they could get a good deal at one of the shops they had passed.

Although the security situation appeared to be improving there had been a clamp down on movement around the city. Everyday business was becoming more restricted and there was still an 11pm curfew. The need for ex-pats was becoming increasingly important as a white face in Iraq made everything easier. I had never experienced such discrimination but the bald fact was that if you were white you had a different queue at check points and it was easier to get onto military establishments. I quickly learned that the key was to have as many pieces of plastic ID hanging around my neck as possible. Whether it was a UK driving licence, my gym membership from London, something I had manufactured myself or ID from one of the bases, the more you had, the more you could baffle the sentry into letting you into the base. It also helped to throw in a line about needing to see Colonel so and so. Basically I was exploiting the sheer size of the forces in Iraq and the lack of experience of the soldiers on the gate. If I seemed confident and looked as if I knew where I was going and what I was doing I soon realised I could sail through without problems. Once inside I would find the contracting office and get myself issued with a proper pass and then go and start pitching for business. The strategy was to get a DHL presence on the bases and this had to be an ex-pat as Iraqis were not allowed to stay inside.

Despite gurgling stomachs we needed to get up north to visit the military camp at Mosul. The 450km journey was not one I was looking forward to. On the way up we passed some vineyards around Balad and I thought it was time to do some wine tasting. We had an amusing 20 minutes attempting to mime wine tasting to some grape pickers who thought we were deranged. Judging by their response, the grapes were only for eating which was probably a good thing as we still had another three hours drive ahead of us. The journey north took us through a more fertile part of the country where the people were semi nomadic living in their Bedouin tents with the mandatory 4x4 jeep parked next to it. There were also considerably fewer monuments to Saddam, until the outskirts of Tikrit, his birthplace. At Tikrit, although all of them were vandalised, the pictures, mosaics and statues lined the roadsides. The majority of them had had the faces shot out but some saw the more traditional type of graffiti added, comedy moustaches and glasses are obviously a favourite the world over. It must have been strange for Saddam to be travelling around the country, witnessing the disrespect that the people would not have dared show three months previously. The rumours were that he was in Tikrit or Mosul where he had considerable support. My thoughts were that a replacement for these monuments needed to be found soon because the people craved a strong and honest leader, but whether this would come from within Iraq remained to be seen. It was clear by June 2003 that the Coalition Forces needed to step away from being the focus for all the Iraqi woes and at least have a titular head in as soon as possible. It had been mooted that perhaps Crown Prince Hassan of Jordan, as a respected statesman who understood the needs of the different groups, would form a constitutional monarchy. However I suspected that this was not a role that was high on his personal agenda. The Iraqi's believed that their leader should come from within and they particularly resented those who fled Iraq during Saddam's time and lived a life of luxury whilst they suffered. Perhaps the solution would come from within but I feared too many vested interests for this to be an easy choice.

We eventually arrived in one piece (just), although not without incident. The Iraqis tended to drive with a numbingly fatalistic attitude. If they had an accident they wrote it off to 'Allah's will' and the result was a total disregard for any kind of highway code, from white lines (not that there were any) to directions in the flow of traffic on the motorway. I no longer found it surprising to see vehicles or donkeys and carts driving towards me on my side of the motorway. The producers of ITV's 'World's worst drivers' would have had a field day, albeit they would not have got any air time in Iraq because it was all regarded as totally normal.

We settled into the camp at Mosul having been informed that shortly before we arrived the ammunition dump had caught fire causing pretty good chaos as rounds cooked off. It resulted in an Iraqi losing an arm and a US soldier losing a foot. Things had soon calmed down and by early evening we were able to enjoy the cooler airs and green countryside. I remembered that it was just north of here that Ishmar, a beekeeper I met during my first week in Iraq, would have brought his bees next month if they hadn't been looted. He used to bring them up for the flowers that could be found with the cooler climate. We had our 'actions on arriving at a camp' down to a fine art now. Having blagged our way through the gate we found the pass office, legitimised our entry and then tried to find somewhere to stay. We ended up sharing a tent with three Chinook pilots who had all been in the army for over 25 years each and had a yarn or two to tell. The topic of the day was shooting at dissidents in the north. There was not a great deal I could add to the conversation so I just nodded and smiled whilst mentally planning the activities for the following day. The next day involved a meeting with the Mayor and his cohorts and we went through a similar process to the one achieved in Baghdad. We hammered the point home by requisitioning one of the Chinook pilots who had used DHL in Afghanistan. Following five minutes of him extolling the virtues of our service, the waverers were converted and they were putty in our hands. Having finessed our pitching methods we replicated this around the country and as predicted in the original strategy paper we were soon to have far more work than we could cope with.

9 PUBLIC RELATIONS

Building good relationships is as much about investing in future good will as it is marketing present activities. A healthy stock of warmth and respect can be invaluable in withstanding the unexpected and preventing negative developments from getting traction in the public arena.

(The Encyclopedia of Current Business Orthodoxy)

I managed to pick up a few souvenirs from the hawkers outside the Palestine. They were selling a variety of Saddam memorabilia from Saddam watches, to guns and the US most wanted playing cards. The crème de la crème were some rather fetching shell suits that had been looted from the Iraqi Olympic team store room. I was able to lay my hands on a couple and sent them to the boys in the UK. I am pleased to say that they went down very well at the local gym. There was not a great deal of opportunity for sport in Iraq and doing something like running or going to the gym would have been regarded as eccentric at best. So instead we managed to locate one of the three bowling alleys in the country - it was under the Palestine. Now this was the kind of sport that they relished, cigarette in one hand and coke in the other. They actually took it very seriously and before long we were almost masters following tuition from the Iraqi champion. Also, before we knew it, our PR machine had been kicked into gear and DHL became accidental but proud sponsors of the Iraqi bowling team who then went on to compete in the Arab cup in Qatar. They were the first Iraqi team to compete internationally since the war and were ably advised by two team 'medics/advisors' from DHL called Phil and Heyrick.

On the golf front we had the first annual 'Drive the Tigris challenge'. The result of a drunken bet by the Kiwi contingent who were confident enough to wager $500 that one of them could drive five balls across the Tigris. I had a club and balls ready for them the next day and that evening we were able to witness the first ball being firmly planted into a bed of reeds ten feet beyond the tree. The second fared slightly better and dropped into the water about halfway across the 350m stretch. A valiant effort and the record to date so if any of you think you can do better, please get yourself out to Baghdad! Later that evening the betting got slightly out of hand and ended up with Phil swimming two lengths under water holding the golf club, lightening the wallet of a Canadian by $1200!

OK, I promise this is the last Bulgarian pilot story. As usual there was a certain amount of gesticulation and shouting when they landed. It transpired that they had flown in using oxygen masks as one of the windows had blown out on the descent. Inevitably the dispute was about the flight home and they quickly confirmed that they would be taking off on schedule as the window would be fixed... in Bahrain. True to their word they kept to the plan and used the oxygen masks all the way back to Bahrain. I delayed my holiday by a few hours until one of the Airbus had landed and had a lift back with them.

I found it fascinating to come back to UK to be told how terrible it was in Iraq. I decided that I must be spectacularly unaware of my surroundings as it did seem as if the corner had almost been turned. Admittedly the odd plane may have been shot at but the one that made the news in June was a total fabrication. The press had missed the story by a week and obviously felt that it was still newsworthy. So they reported that it had happened that night and grabbed themselves a headline. The truth is, things had been improving steadily but the Coalition really needed to get itself an effective PR company as nothing positive was ever reported which merely compounded the problem. This was reflected whilst over on leave when I had an interesting morning at the Arab British Chamber of Commerce. The idea was to have a five minute chat about Iraq with a friend's father. Before I knew it I was presenting Iraq to an ex cabinet minister, various UK corporations and a delegation from Saudi. They seemed keen yet afraid to explore the opportunities. I tried to persuade them that they should follow the lead of companies that had been out there since the beginning, like DHL. Those that were taking the risk were finding that it was paying off considerably. British Airways had been out there for a couple of months and were poised to win flying concessions. However, like the other carriers, there was to be a delay for BA because of the state of the airport which had over two million dollars of damage done to it following its capture.

The cleanup operation was beginning to show signs of success. What's more, of the four terminals, one was almost operational. The other issue they were confronted with was working with or around the various agencies that had control. There were four organisations that believed they controlled the airport. The US Army, the US Air Force, the Civilian contractors and the Civil Aviation Authority. In addition there was the question of where Iraqi Airways and all their employees fitted in. Ironically because I talked to all five groups I had a better idea about what was going on than them as they continued to ignore each other. The process was made all the more awkward by the constant reshuffling going on in the CPA. By July we were on our third civil aviation minister. As each one arrived they took a month to settle in before asking the same questions their predecessor had asked. This lead to a series of ambitious promises, a period of inactivity and then a new minister. Part of the problem was that the ministers that were hurriedly cobbled together post war were very much your Vauxhall league as opposed to Premiership candidates. Admittedly there were some excellent operators but they ended up getting bogged down in the mire that worked with or for them. Getting anything done was slow and painful and the situation was exacerbated by their tendency to contradict their ambitions to authority by referring to one another whenever they were actually called upon to make a decision. Predictably, BA soon got fed up and looked at flying into Basra or leaving altogether and they eventually opted for the latter. The ground handling equipment (most of it French and only a couple of years old) was workable so everything was set for flights; but it was the threat to the aircraft that was the main issue. As a result the airlines began to look at flying into Basra and whilst they were still thinking about it, Richard Branson's Virgin had a plane in there. By road it was an eight hour journey to Basra along a route made of what felt like corrugated iron. The result was a very good impression of a drunkard whenever we stopped and got out of the car to stagger around with shaking knees to pour more fuel into it. It also meant that the locals could pick up most of the supplies bound for Baghdad as they bounced off the back of the military trucks. There were several occasions when we saw Iraqi vehicles that were overflowing with produce and military supplies. They were following the convoys and picking up stuff that had literally fallen off the back of a lorry.

Southern Iraq is hotter, dustier, more barren and poorer than the rest of the country. The Bedouin wander in the distance tending their sheep and goats. The environment is harsh and unforgiving with dunes of fine sand that stretch into the distance. Convoys of military trucks, some up to eighty vehicles long, trundled along the road, kicking up a smog of dust and preventing anyone really seeing what was going on. There were numerous hulks lying at the side of the road that looked like the result of traffic accidents. Eventually we arrived in Basra and I was immediately struck by how poor it is. A town with Iraq's only access to the sea should be thriving. But like Um Qasr down the road, it needed to have its port dredged. This had begun at Um Qasr with the contract being awarded to two dredging companies. There were however three that were operating as a contract had also been awarded before the war. The result was that each company was dredging their part of the port and depositing it into the areas belonging to the other two! Eventually this was sorted out but the opening was further delayed by the local population. They began to demand extraordinary salaries to operate the port. They knew they were the only ones allowed to operate the facilities as they were the last to work there and still laid claim to their jobs. Commercial shipping was unwilling to pay the ridiculous rates and so stale mate resulted, hampering the progress yet further. There was also clear evidence that the Shia majority, who were subjugated under Saddam, had regained their grip. This has had a mixed effect depending on how extreme the local Shia were. In the area where we stayed, for example, a can of Heineken cost $6, three times the price in Baghdad. This was because they were killing the shopkeepers that sold it.

Evidence of the war was all around. All the ground floor windows of shops and hotels/restaurants were bricked up, two holed ships were listing in the harbour and the ubiquitous tank remains littered the roadside. I remembered that these people had experienced the war before and the looting that went with it. This time they were well prepared. We only stayed there a night before heading back up to Baghdad via Ur. Conveniently there was a military camp near by which gave me a rare opportunity to revisit my archaeological studies. I dredged up what I could remember about the site and gave a quick history lesson on Ur.

After only two days away I could feel a marked increase in the nervousness of the Baghdad troops. The body count had been rising alarmingly. I was even accosted by a soldier as I went running next to the runway one morning. He shoved his gun in my face and asked me what I was doing. As I was dressed in shorts and trainers and sweating a lot I thought it was fairly obvious but explained it to him anyway. He seemed slightly mollified and explained that he thought I was going to sabotage a landing plane; an interesting concept. I attempted a wise crack but realized I was going to have to explain myself and it was far too hot to hang around. The nervousness was well founded as the latest Iraqi trick was to lob grenades off bridges into Hum Vs as they passed below; to put rocks/children in the road to slow the drivers down and make an easier target and to put paper bags in the road packed with explosives. The roads were hazardous enough without having to scan the bridges and avoid debris all at the same time!

In spite of these hazards we felt it was time for another trip north to deliver several lorry loads of freight to Mosul and take Kirkuk in for the first time. Some soldiers wanted to come with us so Hernandez climbed into the back of the car. Having discovered that we were not Australian he mentioned that he collected money. I thought I could guess the next question, but then he outfoxed me when he asked for some British currency and some English currency. The man would not stop asking questions. After three hours I crumbled under his torrent of dimwittedness. Seven hours later, I had attempted chewing tobacco (gets stuck in your teeth) and had been talked through his life in Mexico (tequila and whores). The panacea was to repeat our three tapes (Annie Lennox, Crowded House and Rolling Stones) and give him some beer. He slept like a baby or a drunken Mexican, whichever you prefer.

In Mosul our hosts for the night were the 101st Airborne. After a hearty meal of rations, lager and some banter from Hernandez it was time for bed. We had been downgraded from sleeping with Chinook pilots to sleeping in a hangar next to their helicopters. It wasn't the end of the world as since our last visit I still hadn't 'wasted' any dissidents so I probably would have had as little to add to the conversation as before. Apart from a few loud bangs I slept well until they started their singalong PT routine in the morning. I couldn't really understand what they were saying but there must have been half a dozen platoons competing with each other. I was surprised to see that they were also running with their platoon flags. For a second I thought they had clearly been watching too many movies but I quickly realised this was for real.

Another habit I had found difficult to take seriously was the amount of guns and knives these guys carried around with them. I suppose it dates back to the frontiersmen who first settled in the USA. It is clearly deeply rooted in the American psyche and for the first time I understood how massive the American gun lobby must be. Every man and woman had at least two guns and several knives. The latter varied from a small penknife to divers knives strapped to their calves. It was not unusual to see people with two pistols strapped to their thighs, like John Wayne, a huge knife strapped to their calf and all this whilst they were wearing PT kit. It was superb and we used to lay bets on speed and volume by going into a room and asking if anyone had a knife I could borrow. The aim was to guess to the nearest number and the quickest draw. As we drove out of our hangar I noticed four yellow flags stuck in the ground. 'What are those?' I asked a passing soldier. 'That's where the mortars landed last night Sir!' was the reply. Thankfully Amsterdam's finest hadn't resulted in me joining in the panic that we learned had continued throughout the night. I also made a mental note to have some good war stories for the next time we came to Mosul so we didn't have to sleep next to the helicopters again. I remember thinking it was rather foolish to mark the positions of the mortars as we could already see some of the locals sitting on a bank on the other side of the wire watching everything that was going on before them. I called the DHL rep in Mosul the following night and sure enough, they had been mortared again. This time they had improved on their accuracy resulting in some damaged helicopters and some serious injuries. I asked the rep if he wanted to be pulled out but he was more concerned about his air conditioning unit that had been knocked off the side of the portacabin by a Hum V that was fleeing the impact area!

We drove an hour and a half south to Kirkuk the next day and were pleased to discover that they had a swimming pool. Following our sales pitches to the various units on camp we were diverted from our usual routine and jumped into the pool. By the time we thought about accommodation it was too late. So camp beds were erected next to the car. Within an hour we had both been well and truly munched by mosquitos so we gave in to the inevitable and climbed into the car. An hour later we had both sweated off at least a stone, so eventually succumbed and opened the window a crack. The irritating high pitched zzzz of a mosquito heralded the first successful penetration into the car. It turned out to be one of the more painful nights I had experienced in Iraq. However, as a direct result of us spreading the DHL gospel work picked up dramatically and within the space of three months we had established several offices and had seven flights a day into Baghdad.

10 TRAINING

A learning organization is one that adapts and thrives in changing market conditions. But being a learning organization rarely comes naturally. It requires attention and concentration. The rewards, however, are quick to materialise in performance, standards, and morale.

(The Encyclopedia of Current Business Orthodoxy)

Our ex-pat recruitment strategy was leaving a little to be desired. I think the news headlines were doing nothing to help because it was obvious that our HR pipeline had sprung a serious leak and dried up. I must admit it was quite entertaining having to do the hard sell as a potential employer. Words sounded a little hollow when I answered reasonable questions like 'is it dangerous out there?' with statistical comparisons to being run over by a bus. The hiring of Iraqis had also been an interesting experience. The first few were friends of friends and then we got to the stage where the whole family was turning up for work. We tried using an individual who claimed to be a recruitment specialist but it transpired his specialism was in drafting family members, or entirely the wrong people. The airport had begun a strict vetting procedure to decide whether our employees would merit a pass to get them in. It involved a series of questions, the first of which was 'If a stranger asked you to put a package on a plane would you a) put the package on the plane or b) inform your supervisor'. The second part of their vetting was an Interpol search on the persons name to see if they had been caught doing any criminal activity outside the country. This was never likely to prove much as none of them had ever left Iraq. So we put our own strict vetting procedure in place. We would meet the individual, they would do a day's trial and then we would meet the parents. This seemed to do the trick. They were all very keen and totally overqualified as most had engineering degrees. They also had to lie to their neighbours about who they worked for otherwise they would face reprisals.

Once hired, we trained them. The next step was for them to forget the training and proceed to do the job how they thought it should be done! I had been to see the Minister for Justice to speak to one of his lawyers about any pre-existing labour laws that may have survived. It turned out that there were ways that business was done but that it was not exactly law. Also that employee rights were non existent. They could be sacked at will and they need not have any holiday except for religious ones. This, watered down with a large dose of reality, was what I had in the back of my mind for the next time our HR director started questioning me about the employer/employee contract in Iraq. There is a way of working that occurs throughout the region and it is very different to anything I had witnessed before. The reason really lay with the state, which had been the largest employer. There had been very little for them to do and because they were paid so badly they had no inclination to accomplish the smallest tasks. This was an attitude that was very difficult to change. Their working day used to involve coming in at 9am, having breakfast and a cup of tea, having more tea at 11am and then having lunch at 12.30. At 2pm the day finished and they went home. So it was a shock to the system when they came to work for us and needed to be at work by 7am and remained until 7pm. Furthermore, they had to do jobs as individuals, not as a group with one person working and the others advising and smoking. This habit was the hardest to change and if they were left alone for too long they tended to revert to the good old methods. It followed that, an aspect of their work that we found very difficult to instill was a degree of leadership or management. We had four supervisors and twenty workers at the airport. At times there was little to distinguish one from the other. Trying to teach someone delegation and teach the rest of them to have a sense of responsibility and ownership for what they were doing was proving to be a long process. Their whole lives they had been trying to get by without being noticed and now they had had their world dramatically up ended. We were asking them to stand out from the crowd. There were a couple who were on the verge of showing initiative but they would then step back from the brink because of the fear of the unknown. It took time and eventually they began to understand what was required.

All sorts of weird and wonderful modifications were made to the way they were shown how to do business. On one occasion I was watching Mamoon driving his forklift from one end of the area to the other. On one of the blades of the fork was balanced a small box that he could have easily carried. As the fork lift bounced along so did the precariously balanced box. I waved a warning to him before the inevitable happened. He waved back with gusto smiling broadly. The box fell off the blade and went under both wheels. It wasn't until he had driven another 50m that he realised he had lost his precious cargo. He reversed back, squashed it again, picked it up and balanced it on the fork again before giving me a wave and driving off.

The final ingredient to our employee concoction was a Moldovan crew who had replaced the Bulgarians. They were based in our hotel in Baghdad. Their job was to do a daily 'milk run' to the smaller bases to ensure they had a good service. But they were a militant bunch, quite lazy and badly paid. They also realised that they were a scarce commodity. So one morning they announced they were on strike. I went up to their room to find myself surrounded by seven guys in their grubby underpants arguing with me and amongst each other. I thought I was doing fairly well until the navigator asked 'are you married Heyrick?' as he put his hands down the front of his pants. 'Very much engaged was my reply' as I backed towards the door. In the end we managed to persuade them to fly. Part of the reconciliation package meant that later that day and long into the night we were forced to drink rather a lot of vodka with Sergei the navigator and the Captain who was the ring leader and potential gold medal winner of the chain-smoking Olympics.

By the third month we had opened an office in the OCPA (equivalent of Parliament). I had spent a month badgering and persuading various people that the storage room by the front door could be ours. This was key to getting DHL in the minds of those who were running the country (and the contracts) and it helped business no end. It also meant that rather than being outside, where it was too hot for flies, I was able to sit in one of the large palace ballrooms enjoying the aircon, care of Uncle Sam. I brought one of the drivers into the palace one morning and his eyes almost burst out of his head. All he could say was 'why did he (Saddam) do it? Why did he do it?' He was speechless and furious with the blatant waste and abuse of power. It was the first time he had seen what he had only heard about through rumour and he explained that it was far more opulent than he had ever dared to believe. I then joined him on his rounds as I was concerned that he was slow even by Iraqi standards. I soon found out why. Our first delivery was to the Ministry of Defence. The building was closed - in fact it had been flattened by a bomb. The next was to a lady who was also known as Mrs. Anthrax. Her family denied all knowledge of her existence and her neighbours called them liars. Tensions rose so I tried calling the phone number on the package. I misdialed and got through to the detainee facility which was rather ironic and didn't really help matters. They eventually signed for her package and we left with the neighbours gesticulating wildly. It sounds amusing but it highlighted the fear and distrust that was part of every day life and showed why it took so long to get things done.

Time was running out so I went back to the office where I had a message from the rep in Balad camp to say his takings for the week were $79 short. I was rather unimpressed and mentioned this but had to back pedal as he told me the debtor had blown his head off the previous night. His last action before committing suicide was to pack up his box and send it home care of DHL. Later that day I was chatting to a Chaplain who mentioned that he had been tasked to write 'the suicide avoidance pack'. This was because the troops were about to be told that they are going to be out in Iraq for over a year. He explained that it was OK though because they got three days leave in a military camp in Kuwait, once a year. I imagined his pack was in high demand. No wonder the soldiers I came across were disinterested and disheartened. Imagine standing at a checkpoint, wearing body armour and a helmet in the sweltering heat for 12 hours a day. At the end of the day you then went to bed in a tent and repeated the process for a year. Things were due to ease for them about a year later as one of my clients was recruiting and training the new Iraqi army and there was no shortage of volunteers, presumably former conscripts. The clients were living in a village that had been built near the Iranian border to house several thousand troops. It was never completed and remained without windows or doors for 13 years as the German construction firm undertaking the project were never paid. Our client was due to train 40,000 recruits by the end of the year and these would then be filtered out onto the streets to gradually replace the Coalition Forces.

By July we were still living in a hotel in town but were toying with the idea of a move into porta-cabins on the airport so that we could relax a little on the security front and cook our own food. The Flowers Land Hotel had recently added a third dish to its menu. With your bottle of 'Italian French' wine 'brewed in southern France' you could have chicken or meat. With a flourish, Edmundo, the head waiter, told us he was pleased to announce a new dish, 'missed grill.' The missed grill, as he called it, was a combination of chicken and meat which was imaginative. At the beginning of July a new employee arrived, fresh from Ireland. It was the same night that the news broke of the death of Uday and Qusay. November 5th came early as everyone stood on the streets firing their weapons in all directions. So much for the Coalition weapons amnesty the previous fortnight. We were having a meeting in the Palestine and it was time to return to our hotel. There were bullets flying as we hopped into the cars. I was in front and Phil followed as we proceeded to do 80mph down the equivalent of the embankment. It was incredibly dark in Baghdad at night because there was still no electricity and so I could vaguely make out the shapes of people standing by the road firing their weapons. Suddenly there was a burst of automatic fire to my left and tracer whipped between the two vehicles that were no more than ten metres apart. By this stage our man from Ireland was crouched in the foot-well on the passenger's side. Phil explained that the tracer was in fact fireworks but it didn't wash. So he tried a new tack: 'How's your brother getting on these days?' 'Fuck my brother, just get me out of here' was the response, which under the circumstances was reasonable enough. We got back to the hotel and he bolted upstairs wide eyed and scared witless. The rest of the evening was spent reassuring the poor lad that this didn't often happen and that he should give it a few more days before he headed home.

The next morning we heard that a soldier who was watching the tracer from the roof of a building had been killed by a falling bullet. The press the following day had the two prostrate bodies of Uday and Qusay on the front page. It is very much the norm in the Middle East to be far more up front about death so if they have a photo they'll show it. There followed an interesting article about how they were killed. I flipped the paper over and on the back page was a picture of David Beckham at his first training session with Real Madrid, all quite incongruous really. Our Irishman's mental state had improved and he was now able to take a gentle ribbing. I decided to take him to the Zoo. This was the one that was seriously looted. There were a couple of South African guys running it but their background was more safari than urban zoo. Nevertheless they were doing a fantastic job and never slow to spot an opportunity for good PR, DHL were soon flying in a delegation of Zoo keepers to help train the Iraqis. The zoo itself was the sight of considerable fighting during the war and the soldiers had to shoot some of the animals, notably the tigers when their wall was mortared and they started terrorising the soldiers. It must have been strange to see the tigers running around the playgrounds and park that surround the zoo whilst a battle raged on either side of them.

There were two zoos in Baghdad but the second had deteriorated so badly that it had been closed down after the war and the animals moved to the main zoo. It had a staff of 35 but only five of these had any idea what they are doing. Part of the reason for this was that the Zoo was the last stop shop for those that could not find government employment anywhere else and because they were employed by the state they could not be fired. When you think how badly the people were treated you can imagine how the animals were tended. The staff needed to be completely re-educated about the animals they were looking after. In the past they had simply baited them and now they were being asked to nurture them, a concept that was totally alien.

The Zoo was one of Saddam's trophies and this was emphasised when the South Africans were contacted by a man who said that the zoo had ordered some elephants and giraffe. We were shown where they were going to be housed and even to a layman I realised that this was inadequate as it was about the size of a tennis court. In fact, they would have barely fitted through the enclosure gates. At this stage they had a few bears, some birds of prey, pigs, boar, a wolf, lots of dogs (brought by the soldiers) and then there were Uday's animals. Uday had kept his own private zoo to the rear of his palace, on the banks of the Tigris. It contained, amongst other things, big cats and ostriches. At the end of the war they needed to be moved to the zoo and the ostriches were brought from his palace, which was a couple of kilometres away. The soldiers upon whom the task had been bestowed had no means to transport them. They had used their heads and tied the female into the back of a Hum V and the male ostriches chased them down the road all the way to the zoo, which was an amusing sight. The big cats were doped and were also moved via Hum V. The lions and cheetahs were all in good condition and fairly tame as he had clearly doted on them. In a corner, tucked away, was a fairly nervous looking donkey in an enclosure offset from the others. I soon realised the reason for his nervousness as I was told that when they first came here they had nothing to feed the cats so they went and purchased donkeys and slaughtered them for the lions and cheetahs. The latter thought that it was Christmas and New Year rolled into one. As for the former, history failed to recount their thoughts on the matter.

On a more jovial note, in August I celebrated my birthday. The hotel found out and we were shown some of the legendry Iraqi hospitality. Ten of us sat down to dinner. We started with Iraqi champagne, which burns the roof of your mouth and finished with 'the finest two year old Iraqi malt'. The dinner was interspersed/interrupted by 25 frenzied renditions of 'Happy Birthday Mr. Heyrick' by the resident musician who also thought it was great fun to attempt to smother me with kisses. He was so insistent that if I had stayed at supper another hour I would have got a rash from his moustache which would have taken a little explaining. Then, in September I had my first visitor to Iraq. Tim's visit was under the guise of business but actually he just wanted to have a look for himself. A lawyer from the Caribbean, he sampled the culinary delights of the Flowers Land and lived to tell the tale. He also managed some good meetings in the CPA. His opening meeting was particularly memorable. We went in to see the Chief Advocate whose office was one of the many in the ministerial wing of the palace. I walked in and shook hands with him and Tim did the same. For some reason Tim's hand foot co-ordination became inextricably linked and as he put his right hand out his left foot shot out. He connected with a waste paper basket, kicking it across the office, spilling the half empty cups of coffee over the freshly polished marble floor. His natural reaction was to try and pick up the rubbish and shake the man's hand at the same time but it was never going to work and I almost lost control watching him cope with the dilemma. Despite this inauspicious start he did manage to resurrect the situation and make a little sense but I could still see an amused twinkle in the Chief Advocate's eye as we left at the end of the meeting.

As our employees got to know me they began to open up a little more and answered questions about their former life and life in Baghdad today. At times I got more than I anticipated. On one occasion I was quizzing Ziad. Ziad was a well educated middle class guy. His father was in the Air Force and flew cargo planes until the end of the First Gulf War. He had trained in the UK and in Russia and after his days in the Air Force set up his own engineering business. Ziad had a degree in mechanical engineering and was now 28 years old. He got engaged just before the war and had been saving his money to get married in October 2003, but his wedding was delayed because his uncle died and there was the obligatory mourning period of 40 days following a death in the family. Upon leaving university he went to work on a building site, building what was to be the biggest mosque in the world. He left this job at the end of his contract as he said everyone was trying to scam extra money. This resulted in concrete with too much sand in it for the foundations and things of eight feet where they should be ten feet. The site turned into a death trap which, coupled with the total disregard for safety, resulted in a death a week. He was being paid $1 a day. His alternative had been to go into the army. However, his father had paid the government bribe of $1000 to have his service reduced to three months. He then had to pay his local officer another $100 to ensure that he did not have to turn up for those three months. An expensive business when you look at the $30 a month he was earning on the building site. After his three month contract had ended he was due to go to India to further his education but this fell through.

Whilst he was pondering his future, an incident that happened to a friend of his called Haider helped him make up his mind and convinced him that he needed to leave Iraq. Everyone has a story about the regime's brutality and this goes to show how far reaching Saddam's brutality really was. Haider, who was a mechanic, had saved enough money to buy his own taxi. He was working as a courier for an officer in the Passport office. One day he was asked to deliver a passport to a local family. This was to enable the father to travel with his daughter to India, which he duly did. The father returned to Baghdad without his daughter as he feared that Uday was going to take her. It was common practice for Uday to roam the streets in his car pointing out girls that caught his eye and these would then be brought to his palace at night. After a week the neighbours realized that the daughter had not returned and told the secret police who arrested the man, the passport officer and Haider. Haider was taken to a jail in the south east of Baghdad and incarcerated. The building looked normal from the outside but as you walked into it you realised that there was a gentle slope down to about ten metres. The entrance to the jail was very narrow and on both sides were cages for individual prisoners. These actually housed ten men. Further inside were two huge cages that contained the remainder of the prisoners, except for those in solitary confinement. Haider was put into solitary for a week and systematically tortured to find out if he knew what he had been carrying. He had his arms tied and was suspended from the ceiling by his wrists. Electrodes were attached to his earlobes and testicles. Following the torture he had to have one of the testicles removed. One of the more drawn out methods of torture was to tape up his penis and force him to drink water whilst feeding him diuretic tablets. Every 15 days he was allowed ten minutes of exercise in a yard. This lasted for three months and then with no warning at all he was released.

Following these events, Ziad's father sent him to work in Amman without a second thought. He worked for his cousin who was bringing in equipment to Amman for making rockets. It turned out that he was actually smuggling this into Jordan from Russia and then across the border for the Iraqi government. They were also doing the same for spare parts for military trucks. Ziad remained in Amman for two years and returned just before the war. He returned to Baghdad on his last job with seven truckloads of pens for the Ministry of Education. This was at the end of January 2003. During the war the family stayed in the Mansur district of Baghdad with his Aunt. They had been moved out of their house because the Air Force needed to use it. The airfield was behind the house and my guess was that his father was given the house whilst he served as an officer in the air force. His Aunt's home was just round the corner from the home that was destroyed during the war because Saddam was thought to be inside. The locals always knew it was a Saddam safe house because everything about the house was a little too new. It also had different telephone and electrical cables leading into it. Their thoughts were confirmed the week before the bombing when Uday had twice been seen driving in and out of the house.

Throughout the war the family stayed in doors, keeping to the ground floor, hoarding their supplies, as the nightly bombing rocked the city. They felt that the bombing was diminishing in intensity and guessed that the war was drawing to its conclusion. They began to venture outside a little more and on what turned out to be the penultimate day they were in the street when an A10 flew over head. Some men with AK47s appeared and started shooting at the plane. Ahmed, Ziad's father, told them not to but they replied that they were not fighting for Saddam but were now fighting for Iraq. It seemed that even before the end of the war the anti coalition seeds had been sown. Ahmed took his family back inside and two minutes later the A10 bombed the street killing those that had been firing at it. At the end of the war Ziad was sent to help his brother in law who was a duty manager in the Palestine. This was where we bumped into him and how he became our driver for the day and ultimately our senior Iraqi employee.

11 CHARITY

Companies benefit from showing a sense of concern and responsibility for the wider community beyond their immediate stakeholders. It reinforces trust.

(The Encyclopedia of Current Business Orthodoxy)

I had just spent an hour talking about prosthetic ears and was beginning to wonder how on earth I had got into that situation. DHL had sponsored an Operation Smile reconnaissance mission to Iraq. Op Smile is a charity that carries out plastic surgery on children with cleft palates and in the case of Iraq, they were toying with the idea of replacing the ears of those that had had them removed for going absent from the military. For a week I had been looking after ten eminent plastic surgeons as we examined patients and facilities in Basra. Their aim was to assess the facilities and the competence of the Iraqi doctors with a view to returning with a team of their own in six months. The team would then spend ten days operating on children and possibly ears. The principle concern was to ensure that when they left Iraq there was a part of Operation Smile that remained to fill the vacuum. The prosthetic ear solution had come through a US toy company called Hasbro, which had offered to make the ears. These would then be bolted into place and painted. (Questions had been asked about colouring so one of the first challenges had been to find a local artist to paint the ears. I had visions of an Iraqi doing a botch job and lots of multi-coloured ears wandering around Basra, made worse as they started peeling as soon as they were out in the sun.)

Following their visit they were pleasantly surprised about the facilities and the skill levels of the surgeons. The only problem was that the surgeons were using procedures that were 12 years old. There was also a feeling that the mission was a little premature as the security situation in Iraq was far from settled. The British had been doing a good job in Basra working in 55 degree heat, but were beginning to face an increase in the number of attacks against them. As if to back up the team's concerns a car bomb killed a soldier on our second day in Basra. But rather than hiding behind their walls the British simply stepped up the levels of patrols and seemed to be containing the problem. The British troops, like the Americans, were stretched to the limit and it became abundantly clear that CPA needed to get the Iraqi army up and running as soon as possible, to help make the situation more sustainable. The politicians believed this was on the horizon and that by November they would have their New Iraqi Army. However, judging by the state the people organising this were in, the last time I had seen them there was a gulf between what was expected and what was realistic. They were a long way from sorting themselves out let alone training an army. They were so short of supplies that we had just delivered several pallets of loo paper all the way from the USA. I worked out that on average, it is costing them $14 for every visit to the lavatory.

As it turned out the first members of the Iraqi army

appeared in February, only three months late, which was not bad. We had some of them manning the checkpoint outside our accommodation. They arrived in full camouflaged uniform with webbing, helmets and rifles and proudly stood on guard, checking the occasional vehicle as it drove through the check point. The following day their demeanour had slipped somewhat and they had got rid of their helmets and replaced them with baseball caps and had also removed their webbing. Standards slipped yet further when the next day they gave up all pretences and had propped their rifles against the wall and were all seated, smoking and playing cards with their backs to the traffic. You can lead a horse to water but you can't make it drink. This is the sort of attitude and difficulties the CPA were constantly coming across.

For the trip to Basra we had taken the precaution of hiring some security guys from a South African firm that had been in Iraq since the last throes of the war. They really had a few stories up their sleeves. They had been Jay Garner's bodyguards when he had first come out to Baghdad in the last days of the war. Apparently he liked to go out at night and see what was going on for himself. This would often lead to Iraqis shooting at the vehicle and on a regular basis the South Africans stopped and dispatched the aggressors before carrying on the tour of the city.

Whilst down in Basra we had lunch in the Palace and I bumped into a couple of guys I was in the army with. They warned me that there had just been a car bomb and there was some rioting on the route we were due to take to our next hospital and they gave me their take on the situation. They felt everything was more or less under control, allowing for the odd anti coalition attacks and said that things had calmed down since the killing of the Royal Military Policemen. The big difference in Basra was that the locals were actively supporting the British and helping make it more difficult for the anti coalition forces to operate.

On the Op Smile team's last day we flew up to Baghdad in the DHL executive plane. It sounds very grand but actually was a modest affair that looked like a cigar tube with wings. It was also like a sauna. Once in Baghdad I took the team up to the CPA palace and we went and had 30 minutes with Mr. Bremer. Now there was a man under pressure; under pressure in the media, from Washington and from the Iraqis to deliver tangible results. Compounding the situation, he also had terrorist activity causing problems across the country. He was desperate to get things done but seemed hamstrung. At the time the most recent example had been the UN bombing (the US military had offered to guard the building and set up some defences but the offers were turned down). Following the explosion the military came under the spotlight and received a large portion of the blame. I had been to the building on several occasions and the UN had employed local security guards and had minimal defences outside. I expect they felt that they were unlikely to be a target but in an environment that saw indiscriminate attacks and bombings this proved to be a poor assessment. The bomb actually went off when I was on leave. The same day I had to go in and see the DHL insurance company in London and present the security situation to them with the ambition of persuading them not to increase the bill for our aircraft. Following my presentation I discovered that they were going to increase our bill by 20% a day after a risk assessment that was based entirely on what they had seen on the news. Thankfully they listened and froze the increase indefinitely.

As I was leaving the building and feeling quite pleased with myself I received a call from Baghdad saying that leaflets had been distributed throughout the city to workers with foreign companies telling them that they would be shot - not great for work force morale. But a combination of the dollar and the fact that our employees had lived their whole life under threat, meant that things quickly returned to normal. Also, the alternative for our employees was for them to sit at home as they had done since they had left university. They were certainly not going to let a job slip through their fingers when they were in such short supply.

Life appeared to be relatively cheap in Iraq and threats came in abundance. One Monday Ziad was driving through town when he was cut up in the traffic and got into an argument with a guy who said he was the son of the acting Minister for Defence and promptly put his pistol to Ziad's head. Fortunately he was dragged away. A policeman on the scene told Ziad he was not going to press charges because it would be more trouble than it was worth. Ziad also discovered that the policeman was a relative of Saddam, had served in the secret police and now worked for the Coalition. It was not an uncommon story and although it looked like everything had changed to the outside world the reality was that much was, as our Iraqis would say, 'same-same'. It would be naïve to expect a complete purging of the government and secret police because actually these were people who knew how to run the country.

The fact that Saddam had gone alleviated much of the suffering that had been widespread. There were countless examples of the former regime's brutality that affected every employee. I was chatting to a couple of them one day and once they started they really began to open up. Mohammed's father was a General in the army and when he retired was asked to join the Ba'ath party. He refused and a month later was admitted to hospital. He died from 'cancer' two days later following a dinner at the local base. Ma'moon left the army following completion of his national service and went to university. Having completed his first year where he got straight A grades he was then asked to rejoin the army but refused. He promptly 'failed' the year and had to re-sit twice. He explained the reason for not rejoining was because the average soldier got paid $2 ½ a month. If you were a Colonel you got $50 but, Saddam's bodyguards got $50,000 a month. I would imagine the bodyguard rate increased somewhat following the end of the war. Certainly Saddam had no shortage of funds. We were told that a few days before the war Uday turned up at the banks with three articulated lorries and personally oversaw the emptying of the vaults. By August, Saddam was believed to be in the area around Tikrit where there were plenty of high ranking Ba'ath party members. The story floating around at the time was that a butcher was approached by some men and asked if he would come with them to slaughter a goat. He was blind folded and driven for an hour where he then performed the task. He had just finished his work when he felt a hand on his shoulder and an unmistakable voice thanking him. He looked up and saw Saddam standing next to him. Before he could say anything he was then blindfolded and taken back to his shop.

12 TIME MANAGEMENT

Time is a precious and elusive commodity for senior managers. Efficiency requires an accurate account of every minute of the day and the ability to estimate precisely the length of time needed for each and every task. Proper appreciation of this truth can be epiphanous for even the most successful of managers.

(The Encyclopedia of Current Business Orthodoxy)

I was sitting in Sergei's Antonov 12 on my way to Mosul and thought that I would try and answer the question I was often asked about the detail of my daily existence. So at risk of sounding a bit like Adrian Mole, I selected a typical day in October that went something like this:

I was woken up at 5.15am by the roar of the generator outside the hotel kicking into life, the aircon wheezing and the lights flicking back on. The generator was a huge diesel engine that belonged to a train before it found itself acting as an irritatingly reliable alarm clock. I got up in the hope that I would be able to get some emailing done but unsurprisingly the satellite was playing up. BBC World became a reliable second option and I caught a repeat of a program about the world's greatest leaders with Mo Mowlem extolling the virtues of Winston Churchill.

By about 6.15am Sergei and the rest of the crew had eaten a boiled egg (chilled) or 'omlette' (fried egg) and eight of us then squeezed into the jeep and set off for the airport. The airport road was known as bomb or sniper alley but I found that the baddies liked a lie in, so the early mornings were incident free. On the way down, we'd drive past a few tired looking GIs lounging around on their tanks and some Iraqi policemen who were loitering around under a bridge which had been the location for previous attacks. Believe it or not there was a slight nip in the air. Daytime temperatures had only been reaching about 38 degrees.

On arrival at the airport there was the usual queue of trucks, their drivers and other traders drinking tea, praying or just watching the world go by whilst waiting to get in past the soldiers. We met up with our trucks and Iraqis and then escorted them through the checkpoint. This saved them a two hour wait as TCNs (third country nationals) had major difficulties getting through check points. The pilots were then dropped off at their Antonov where they began their routine safety checks - a quick kick of the tyres and a stroll around the plane to ensure that all the holes and leaks were present and correct prior to it being loaded. In the meantime I attempted to get onto the internet to see what the flight schedule was for the day but the CIA were up early and the signal was blocked. The CIA had started to use the same frequency as the DHL satellite, so we needed to buy another one if we wanted email access. I wandered outside to use the satellite telephone and have a quick chat with Pete from Bahrain flight dispatch about what we might be able to expect today. Pete was his usual vague self but assured me that the first plane would land at 9am, just as I saw our first airbus circling to land. It was 7.30am. I wondered why I even bothered to make the call as this was the same guy who told me one morning that there would be no flights because of flooding in Baghdad. At the time I was standing on the runway with the soles of my boots melting. I thanked him for his help and put the phone down, waited 30 seconds, adopted a different voice and called the same number again. I asked him to put me onto another dispatcher. It turned out that we had four Airbuses coming in (upwards of 120 tonnes) and the Antonov was doing its internal milk run to Mosul, Kirkuk and Tallil. Our other bases, Balad and Tikrit would be taken care of by the trucks.

By now it was about 7.45am and the routine began. It was time to drive the high-loader up to the plane and the pallets of mail, aid and commercial freight were pushed out of the plane onto the platform. We had just managed to secure permission to operate the old Iraqi Airways ground handling equipment. This was a major coup. It allowed us to self handle and prevented us from being fleeced by the firm that was bidding for the handling contract and wanted to charge us $7000 to unload each plane. I now classed myself as an expert (I had been driving a high loader for a day) and so was giving the staff a quick lesson so that they could take the helm. I'd imagine that airport regulations in the UK would have required a lengthy course and some sort of health and safety certificate, but this was Baghdad. Whilst I was up there I took the opportunity to have a cup of tea and a chat to the crew to make sure that they were happy with the security situation. It also gave me a chance to answer any questions they had regarding the latest rumours that may have been conjured up by the press. It was essential that they were well informed as otherwise they wouldn't fly and having three airbus sitting in Bahrain would have been quite an expensive hobby.

At about 8.30am I headed up into town to the CPA for a meeting with the Minister for Health about some prospective DHL sponsorship and we organised a game of tennis for the following week. I was slightly late as the coalition forces had put in an extra roadblock during the night. It channeled me through a slalom of concrete barriers before I could get off the motorway. I also touched base with the Minister for Justice in a bid to get an answer on DHL's legal position vis a vis commercial business in Iraq. Ironically we had contracts with USAID and the military and CPA but they were against us providing the service directly to the Iraqis, fearing it would compete with the non existent postal service.

By now it was 11.30am and I returned to the airport to see how things were getting on down there. The barrier to our part of the airport was down. I asked the soldier why and he replied that he didn't know but that he did know that I couldn't go in. I borrowed his radio and had a chat with his sergeant who told me there was a suspect package in the mail hangar. My next thought was the safety of our staff. It transpired that none of the 28 DHL staff or the Airbus crew were aware of the threat so I took action myself and told the soldier not to shoot me because I was going to walk past his barrier and clear the area of my employees. Everyone was evacuated from the office. The plane taxied out for departure and we went and sat by the runway behind some shipping containers and waited for the bomb disposal guys to do their thing. After a couple of hours they declared that the vibrating package was indeed a vibrator that had been sent out to one of the military girls and with a grin we all went back to work.

At about 2pm I headed over to the control tower, run by

the Australian air force, and had a cup of tea and a chat and talked through any security issues that DHL needed to be aware of. There were reports in the media in October of missiles being launched at the planes but the majority were false alarms. Every report, however, became occasion for a lengthy conversation with the aircraft company in Brussels who were very concerned about the appropriateness of flying. Clearly they were torn between the money they were making and the risks they were taking. So, having got the all clear I made a few calls to make sure everyone was happy before hopping on the quad bike and heading across the runway back to the office.

Once there, I had a call from our man in Tallil who told me that the ammunition dump was raided last night by some Iraqis. I didn't think they could have carried much and it was unlikely that they had driven onto the base. So I asked how they got away with it, he went on to explain that a hole had been cut in the fence and a covert team of Iraqis plus donkey had sneaked in and out. Bearing in mind there were 15,000 troops on the base, this was either a feat of staggering bravery or stupidity. I would argue the latter as the troops did rectify the situation the following morning. They simply followed the donkey's tracks for a couple of miles until they led to a house. Inside the house were some sleepy Iraqis and a whole lot of ammunition.

Later in the afternoon there was a knock on the door and a couple of Canadian friends came in. 'Killer' as one of them was called was looking rather nervous and slightly pale and asked if we knew how he could get a flight out of Baghdad. This sudden desire for an exit stemmed from the unwelcome discovery on returning home the previous evening of their security guards and staff tied up and the place ransacked. There had been some shooting but no one was injured. For 'Killer' enough was enough and he decided it was time to head home. He needed 72 hours notice to get on the plane which meant that we had another guest staying with us at the hotel. That was until we heard reports that our hotel had been bombed, prompting 'Killer' to break out in a cold sweat. As with all rumours that floated around I would start by checking as many websites as possible to find more detail. In this case there was not much more than the fact that it was where NBC were staying and a quote from a senior policeman who said: 'It was a small bomb, because if it had been a big one it would have destroyed the whole building' - another brilliantly incisive piece of detective work. As it turned out, the initial reports had been wrong and it happened at the other end of town.

By 4pm we still had two more planes to come in which kept us busy until about 7pm when it was time to head back to the hotel. Just as we were due to leave the email sparked back into life, having been frozen for the past two hours. It delayed our departure for another hour, as it provided an opportunity that couldn't be missed. It was dark now, a bad time to travel, so Phil and I went in convoy back into town. About halfway through the journey, whilst on the phone to Anna, there was a large bang and flash on the road ahead of us followed by some tracer fire and total confusion. Everyone tried to turn around at once and drive in the opposite direction to the oncoming motorway traffic. Rather calmly, I thought, I told Anna I'd call her back and manoeuvered the car behind as many Iraqis as possible. After ten minutes or so all seemed quiet and we edged forward. I put my foot down and lead the charge past the incident point. As I drove past the scene I found that by hunching my shoulders, shrinking down in my seat and avoiding looking at the blown up Hum V it made me feel much safer. We made it back to the hotel in record time and had a couple of beers whilst boring everyone with our tales of bravery.

A handful of newcomers had arrived at the hotel and I introduced myself. The type of people who came out to Iraq come in various guises. The worst were the Walter Mittys. They were the ones who turned up when the situation had calmed down a little but was still short of being totally benign. They then proceeded to shoot their mouth off about all the other world hot spots they had been into first. These newcomers were in that category and promptly gave me a quick lecture on Iraq. I rose to the bait and explained that we had been there for several months. I was astounded when they continued in the same vein, giving me their wealth of experience on their first day in country. At this point, the thought of doing some emails actually became appealing and I headed off to tackle them again. Just as I approached the lift I realised that I had let my guard slip and I heard a 'Mr. Heyrick?' 'Yes that is him', the hotel staff sung out in unison as I feigned deafness. The Iraqis adore a good meeting and many of these came at the end of the day. They used to sit in ambush on the sofas in reception waiting for me to go and have supper. The reasons for the meeting were often unclear but usually involved a 'fantastic deal' for DHL, which required us to give them all our money for little in return. I tried to explain that I didn't really like these deals but they viewed DHL as a potential cash cow and wouldn't be swayed so they would try and grab me most evenings and seduce me with a worse deal than the previous evening. That evening it was a variation on a familiar theme; a man who wanted us to use his trucks. I asked him for his prices saying I already had the cheapest company in the market. He asked me who they were. I made up a name and he proceeded to make up a few stories about them. I thanked him for his time and explained that I wouldn't be using his new fleet of Volvo trucks whether they were painted in DHL yellow or not. I actually had a strict policy on the truck front and used local trucks, the ones that were decorated with whistles, bells and tiger skin carpet on the dashboard. These were ideal as they were cheap and blended in really well. The trucks that were new and expensive tended to be the ones that got ambushed or simply blown up. The second man of the evening wanted me to go to Vietnam for him as the triads owed him $300m. I politely explained that I had enough on my plate at the moment and asked him to send me details. At this point I got up and I managed to nip back upstairs and settled into a spot of BBC World until the electricity cut out at 11pm and forced me to bed.

13 COMPETITION

Understanding the competition, their products, and their strategy is fundamental to success. You can't compete with the unknown. Market research and competitor information are often treated lightly when times are good but it is usually too late to make a difference when conditions get tough. Complacency is fatal.

(The Encyclopedia of Current Business Orthodoxy)

There are lots of factors that mould the way in which companies do business and one of the most important is the competition. Our competition in Iraq was limited due to the perception the competitors had of Iraq. There were some half hearted attempts with local companies being given agency rights but these never really developed into too much of a threat. Instead the main threat came in a totally different form. It manifested itself in the general security situation and it was this that presented the greatest threat to our operations.

Ramadan certainly started with a bang. We had our DHL pre Ramadan party in the Hotel for all the employees. On the other side of the Tigris, the Al Rashid Hotel experienced a different start to Ramadan as several rockets slammed into the side of the building. 'The Queen's Band' had been hired, as had 'Basra' our local guitarist from... Basra - the man of the infamous 'Happy Birthday Mr. Heyrick'. Even as everyone was coming in he was belting out D.I.S.C.O. Iraqi style. This involved shouting each letter followed by bellowing DISCO, DISCO, DISCO. Some might call it repetitive but for pure entertainment it was difficult to top. However, the party almost had to be postponed because the hotel lift was up to its usual tricks. The lift was one of those small two-man lifts, great for an intimate ride with a beautiful girl but not ideal for Heyrick, Phil, Jo and Rado our Air Sofia representative. Rado weighed in at 180kg and so when we got into the lift and pressed G we plummeted down and barely had time to claw desperately at the walls as they flashed past. It felt like I was in a B rate horror movie. Fortunately the lift did stop although by this stage we had overshot the ground floor. To Rado's embarrassment, we needed a ladder to climb out.

Despite our late arrival, the dancing was soon in full swing. Interestingly, this was only for the guys, with the girls simply refusing to participate. The one exception was a half Egyptian girl, who was happily swinging on the dance floor. The other girls watched her with a mixture of envy and disapproval, regarded her as brazen and looked down on her from that day forward. The whole place of women in society really did vary from one situation to the next. For example the girls began to change their dress at work and come to work wearing a variety of western clothes. Some interesting combinations were paraded and were complimented by copious amounts of make up. The boys were fairly dismissive and told me it is only because they are looking for husbands. This was quite possibly true - one of them was dating a pilot (they saw each other every other day in the privacy of the cockpit of the plane). There was an occasion when I suggested that we got everyone together for a beer after a particularly hard day. The largest office was occupied by six girls. Without a thought Ziad marched in, hoofed them out into the cold and told them to wait in the car until we had finished a drink. The boys, however, are the same as boys the world over because for all their dismissiveness of the girls they didn't hesitate to jump when they were asked to do something by them. However, when it came to the dancing at the party the boys took centre stage and certainly enjoyed themselves right up until the curfew.

Meanwhile, two miles across the river the Al Rashid was under rocket attack. This was the one five star hotel in Baghdad. There were many that claimed to be five star, but this was as near as they got and as a result it had been taken over by the Coalition and was filled with senior military and politicians. The Al Rashid episode provided a rude awakening to my first day back from leave. There was only one soldier killed, a Colonel, but it turned out that 12 of the rockets that were aimed at the building failed to fire and the damage might well have been much worse. As for the ICRC and police station bombings, the local Iraqis were distraught. Our foreman had two cousins that were at the police station and found themselves on the critical list. Once again, Iraqis working for western companies were warned to stay at home by the opposition forces. At least whilst Saddam was around they were safe but now they felt threatened even when they were anywhere but inside their houses.

I mentioned that there were certain things that had not changed since the departure of Saddam. The personalities involved in the running of the country had re-emerged in similar roles for the CPA. What I did not expect to hear was that the CPA had been mimicking the state that they rid Iraq of seven months ago. A week earlier two of our employees arrived in the morning looking upset. The previous day Coalition Forces had raided Mohammed's house whilst he was sitting in the garden having tea with his father. The whole family was handcuffed on the lawn and forced to lie on the ground with guns to their head. They were then temporarily arrested and all their money and gold was taken. (Due to the lack of banks they all kept their entire savings at home). The second, Ziad, saw his uncle arrested and the troops taking his entire savings of $100,000 and throwing him in jail. He was a merchant and was arrested for making donations to the Baath party, something he had to do if he was to maintain his business. He was left in jail and in both cases the coalition denied taking the money. After telling me the story, Ziad said mournfully 'this is our freedom'. No doubt there were two sides to the story but I do believe that there was a naivety and desperation on behalf of the Coalition. When someone came and told them that the people living in house X were members of the Baath Party they reacted swiftly and arrested them. What they failed to do was corroborate the information and take into account the petty jealousies and arguments that would have led to these vindictive accusations. It was an impossible task. They had people working for them who were paid to give them this information. There were undoubtedly times when the information was wrong as the informers were under pressure to provide a steady stream of people to inform on. Having arrested the supposedly guilty parties and taken their money they were thrown into jail where they would languish for several months before being released. This was an entirely pointless exercise and it was hardly surprising that support for the Coalition began to wane. This is exactly what would happen in the days of Saddam.

In spite of this the guys remained remarkably sanguine. Moreover, when the Iraqis were killed through the bombings, rather than blame the Coalition for not controlling the situation, they blamed the insurgents who they believed were from Syria. Proof lay in a Syrian who was captured attempting a suicide bomb at another police station shortly after the bombing of the ICRC. Outside that police station, in the west of Baghdad, two film crews were also detained. They were waiting at the scene following a tip off. As you can imagine, the esteem with which I held some journalists reached new depths when it emerged they had failed to pass on the tip in their quest for a scoop. Another example of the twisted coverage of the situation occurred one night when we were sitting on the roof of our hotel. Three mortar rounds whistled overhead and landed in the green zone, around the CPA. They landed with a bang in the unpopulated area away from the palaces. This was about half a mile away from where we were sitting. In case more were fired, we dashed off the roof to find some hard cover and went downstairs to see BBC World interrupt the news and announce that six massive explosions had rocked Baghdad. I know they were under pressure to make the story interesting but those were blatant exaggerations and quite frankly lazy reporting as it was easier to sensationalise explosions than it was to report a good news story.

The bombings of the Al Rashid and ICRC really made the administration sit up and realize that the problem was far more than just some disaffected Iraqis having a crack at the occupying forces. It would have especially hit home when they were moved out of their hotel into enormous dormitories and tents. The morning after the Al Rashid bombing I met the aviation minister coming out of the VIP lounge of the airport. Looking decidedly ropey he explained that he had eschewed the tents in favour of the 'sofa plan' which had not been quite as comfortable as he first envisaged. There is nothing like an uncomfortable night to focus the mind! As a result of the bombings, the security forces began to flap like mad and more concrete blocks were erected daily, doubling journey times around town. Speaking to the soldiers they were itching to get out. I didn't blame them. They were sitting targets and on places like the road to Fallujah one in three military convoys was being attacked. I know they were paid to be soldiers but their odds on survival were severely reduced. As I tuned into forces radio I heard an advert, sponsored by the government, telling fathers to spend more time with their daughters. There was more than a little irony considering the military had just been told that they were on standby to stay in theatre for an extra three months.

14 PEER REVIEW AND FEEDBACK

An objective assessment of performance and process can be valuable in improving the way individuals and entire business units operate. On an individual basis this means feedback from a peer or a manager. On a company level it might involve employing a consultancy to review operations.

(The Encyclopedia of Current Business Orthodoxy)

Dominic, a friend of mine took the opportunity to visit and it was while reading his account of his day in Baghdad that I realised how 'normal' the abnormal had become. A Merrill Lynch fund manager, he needed an excuse to come out so I organised a meeting with the finance minister. We also took the chance to visit the zoo. An Arabist, he speaks flawless Arabic and the girls in the office all went misty eyed over my friend from England who spoke like an Egyptian. Life at the zoo had improved dramatically in the two months since my last visit, from little things like the porcupines having a new enclosure to the open sores on the bears clearing up because they could roam about a bit more. The lions were looking better, especially one of the females who had recently munched the fingers off a drunk GI who stuck his hands through the railings. Whilst we were there we had our own entourage of children all following their new Egyptian friend. No matter how many times he told them he was a Pension Fund Salesman from London they still insisted on asking him about his life in Egypt. Rather than talk about his visit I think the following extract from his diary provides an interesting insight into his views on the country. There are all kinds of details that he has picked up on that I came to regard as normal.

MAY I SMOKE? - 1ST OCTOBER 2003

'Fancy coming to Baghdad for the day?' read the email. Heyrick was suggesting travelling in the 'jump seat' of one of the DHL planes that ferry parcels between Bahrain and Baghdad. The land routes are notoriously dangerous, and though the threat of surface-to-air missiles is as present as ever, it could hardly be as risky as driving for 12 hours from Amman or more than double that from Kuwait through provinces whose populations may or may not appreciate visitors treating their country like a safari park, especially visitors from one of the occupying powers.

I would not be taking the risk for the sake of it. I would not have done a similar trip to a war zone in a region I knew nothing about. As one of the ancient capitals of Arab civilisation, and until recently an important centre of the Arab World, it is a city every Arabist dreams of visiting, not to mention its current relevance to east-west relations and world stability. A quick phone call to the Head of Security at Merrill Lynch, resulted in me being taken through a stack of sobering thoughts. He then admitted he wanted to come too. Most importantly, Heyrick's view was that it would be 'fine' but sensibly did not offer a stronger opinion than that.

I arrived at Bahrain airport at 3.30am and despite Heyrick's precise instructions as to what to do, security wouldn't let me through without a boarding pass, passport control wouldn't let me through until I'd paid the departure tax, the only souls in the check-in desks were either asleep, had mops in their hands or were asleep with mops in their hands and no one individual had a comprehensive solution. When I got to tarmac level at Gate 16A the doors to the outside were locked but moments later the Russian crew of the DHL plane going to Bagram bundled out of the lift and agreed to take me on their transport to the DHL terminal. I'm sure the irony of having Russian pilots dropping off packages rather than anything else was not lost on the Afghans.

I waited a few minutes in the DHL office before Airport Services took me to the Airbus plane destined for Baghdad. Boarding the plane I met the Belgian pilot and first officer as well as Martin the British flight engineer. Martin had trained in the RAF and explained to me that the first we would know of any missile fired at us, if anything, would be a loud bang as an engine or other part of the aircraft exploded: naturally there were no detection devices on an Airbus filled with cargo. The load manager, another Belgian, accompanied us to Baghdad but was only too glad to let me travel on the 'jump seat' in the cockpit, allowing him to catch up on sleep out back.

Steve, the British ground engineer, told me about his recent trip to New York by Concorde with his 79-year-old mother. If only he'd stopped there. He proceeded to tell me about how long the plane had been US (unserviceable) until days earlier and how the other Airbus 'Lima Romeo' was stuck in Baghdad waiting for its undercarriage to be fixed (the only jack broke while they were trying to repair a tyre).

We took off without incident, followed the coast of Saudi Arabia to Kuwait City, then over Basra in a straight line to Baghdad. A DC-10 about 1,000 feet above us was pointed out to me, which prompted Martin to suggest that, during our descent, I keep my eye open for the many US helicopters patrolling Baghdad International Airport. To minimise the risks of flying over insecure parts of the country the captain stayed at 33,000 feet until the last minute, when he began a steep descent. Two unfinished palaces in the middle of a lake just to the east of the airport came into view. Air Traffic Control posed no problems despite its reputation and we landed cleanly on one of the main runways (avoiding the taxiing lanes unlike one unfortunate pilot a few days earlier).

We drew up alongside Lima Romeo, mournfully nursing her crumpled claw. The load manager swung open the doors revealing Heyrick's distinctive figure driving the unloading machine towards us. The low humidity was a welcome change to Bahrain, and it was damn good to see Heyrick after what, in hindsight, proved to be the most frightening part of the day, that flight in. It was difficult to judge the risks from poor serviceability of the aircraft, surface-to-air missiles (SAMs), unconventional landing techniques, our being a soft Western target in a military conflict. I did know there was no turning back. The pilot and his crew were taking me in as a favour so my role was to keep quiet and find out what had actually happened well after any problem had been resolved. Or not. I found myself assigning significance to the body language and even minor changes of expression in the faces of the crew. If they all reacted at the same time I knew it was a reaction to something heard over the radio; if the captain gasped I would assume it was serious; if the flight engineer addressed the captain I'd watch the latter's reaction like a hawk. An index finger pointing at a dial, eyes meeting followed by a giggle and a shrug of the shoulders were more difficult signals to interpret. Warning sounds and red flashing lights may have been silenced quickly but the full ramifications of what they'd been indicating were difficult to guess.

On the ground, Heyrick introduced me to the very friendly Moldovan crew of the 35-year-old Antonov, which spends the majority of its time shuttling between Baghdad, Tikrit, Kirkuk, Mosul and Basra. An unenviable remit, especially the Mosul leg and particularly in a plane that belonged in a museum. Their priority was to get back to the hotel downtown as quickly after the day's flying as possible to get drunk enough early enough to allow them to sleep long enough before their horrendously early start each morning. Heyrick tends to drive them into town to ensure their continued loyalty. They had apparently replaced the Bulgarian crew of underpant fame.

Heyrick introduced me to Ziad, a DHL employee, charming and full of energy even at that time in the morning, and whose words to me were the first I'd ever heard in the Iraqi dialect. It sounded very exotic and had a strange lilt to it but was just close enough to other Gulf dialects not to inhibit communication. Moments later I got my first glimpse of the lovely Yasmin but Heyrick was not around to introduce me... a far cry from the surprisingly numerous woman soldiers of the US Army.

The bulletproof jeep was loaded up with parcels and boxes in the middle of which sat Terrence from Limerick. When the three of us were aboard there was no sign of 'Tel' at all, and the US soldiers at the numerous checkpoints had no clue he was there. Not having the correct papers I wondered if I should have been the one travelling in the back but it would have more than hindered my view, and I have a feeling that, paradoxically, hiding the guy with the right papers was actually a smarter move when all contingencies were taken into account. In any case, at the first checkpoint I flashed my driving licence which, according to Heyrick, would suffice because it was plastic and had a photo on it regardless of what the words say or what authority issued it.

The notorious airport road had a central reservation full of ashes where the Americans had burnt the flora to stop Iraqis hiding there, and for large stretches of it they had built a high concrete wall for protection, a wall reminiscent of the one the Israelis are building in the occupied West Bank, and performing a similar function in that very few Iraqis are allowed close to the airport (except detainees). Soon after we found ourselves on the road that had been the scene of the failed attempt on Uday's life in December 1996.

The Coalition Provisional Authority has set up camp in Uday's palace, just where the Tigris turns north in the centre of town. There are corridor after corridor of 'ministries' with signs printed on sheets of A4 and stuck to the wall with sticky tape. Peering into any of the doorways revealed rows of quiet Americans tapping away on laptops. Peering into a staircase would more often than not reveal a sleeping GI, though apparently in the early days of the occupation the corridors themselves were littered with sleeping soldiers. There was even a barber sitting expectantly in one room though I got the feeling he'd have been taken off guard if you had asked for anything other than a 'number one'.

Walking around this inconceivably large palace the Iraqis had the downtrodden look of an occupied people, averting their eyes from yours to look at the floor as they mopped it. However, as soon as they heard Arabic their faces would light up and the stories would start flowing. Arabic brings with it a code of conduct and a body of shared knowledge, which may have encouraged people to tell stories. They might not have bothered telling someone fresh from North Carolina.

Heyrick led the way to the Ministry of Finance where he introduced me to a man wearing a T-shirt with the words US Embassy Abu Dhabi emblazoned across it called Richard Bloom. It turned out the T-shirt was the result of a mix-up at the laundry and in fact Bloom had recently retired from the Bank of America after 30 years' service before being invited to Baghdad by the US Department of Trade to go to Iraq. Our conversation was always going to be a tricky one. Was I to open with: 'After you have paid back that $300bn of outstanding debt, would you be looking to appoint external managers to manage your reserves and if so, what kind of duration would you be looking for? We feel it would be prudent to have exposure to the Euro within the context of your planned zero trade flows with Europe.' In the event, he launched into an explanation of how they were setting up trade finance institutions separate from the central bank and other public sector banks to avoid having funds snatched by legacy creditors.

In return for his time, Heyrick awarded Bloom a DHL T-shirt to replace the one lost in the laundry and a discount on the next package he sent home by DHL. In the DHL office on the ground floor of the palace I was introduced to Shayma, who told me how she daren't tell her friends and neighbours that she works at the CPA. She confided that she was sure Heyrick was still annoyed with her after some bullets were found in a package she thought (and had told him) she had checked. Heyrick assured her she had been forgiven but that didn't bring back the sleepless nights. Shayma was hoping her American boyfriend will get her out of Iraq before too long. We left Tel to deliver the fresh load of parcels around the CPA and took the jeep back through the checkpoints before heading for the Palestine Hotel. Thankfully we got a call soon after warning us that a demonstration outside it was turning nasty.

We decided instead to grab an early lunch at the Flowers Land Hotel, allowing me to see Heyrick's living quarters and meet the predominantly Christian staff there. They were clearly very fond of Heyrick. Then off to the zoo where Brendan, a South African animal lover, was busy trying to improve the lot of the inmates there. No doubt feeling only slightly less liberated than the Iraqis, the animals had been cooped up in completely inappropriate conditions and the only animals left after the looting were the dangerous ones. It was clear that Uday's animals had received much better treatment than anyone else in the country even if his cheetah had developed arthritis. Strangely, the animals seemed very aware of the difference between a westerner and an Iraqi. If an Iraqi were to approach, some animals would jump up at the bars and roar or bark whilst a westerner could approach and stroke it. That is not to say that some Westerners had not abused that trust. As reported in the press, a drunk US soldier lost a couple of his fingers to a lion he had teased and taunted through the bars. His companion shot the lion dead and the injured soldier was flown off to Germany for surgery. The blood had not been cleaned off the bars of the cage, and in the next cage the dead lion's father paced up and down, oblivious to his son's horrible demise. Brendan has lodged a complaint with the military authorities.

A group of about five children, around the age of ten, toured the zoo with us, and though they had their moments, I for one enjoyed their company. They were clearly too young to understand that, though I spoke like an Egyptian, I was from England so I gave up trying to explain. Say hello to Egypt when you get home! Are clothes expensive in Egypt? Did you buy that watch in Egypt? Brendan finally lost it when they offered a monkey a lit cigarette and I stepped in for the dressing down. They were clearly in the habit of bating the animals and I was distressed to see that when Brendan was looking the other way they would spit on and tease the animals. Maybe all children do that but certainly in a country where the weak have been picked on for so long their behaviour did not surprise me. Though they were desperate for attention, I felt them to be less insistent than their Egyptian cousins would have been in a similar situation. For some reason they kept asking us to watch them swim. When I finally capitulated, Farah, a Christian Iraqi friend of Brendan's, stepped in explaining that a child had drowned not long before in exactly the same spot. Just as the tour of the zoo was coming to an end there was an explosion nearby, which moved the children to tell me how scared they were at night when people were regularly getting shot: one of them holding two fingers up to another's head to make the point. Another of them took me by surprise when, lit cigarette in hand, he asked me 'May I smoke?' I muttered a few platitudes about the hazards of starting so young and he frowned. Health was hardly a priority in Saddam's Iraq, I thought, but then realised he had merely been asking my name, in Iraqi dialect: 'Ma ismak?' So much for my language skills. Dogs, which didn't seem such a rarity in Baghdad to warrant a place in the zoo, inhabited a number of the cages but Brendan explained that some GIs had adopted dogs and had asked him to look after them until they were able to ship them back to the States. Not by DHL I hope. The looting had left lots of spare cages so it was no bother, and the US Military had been generous towards the funding of the zoo.

We got lost on our way out. We knew we had to return to the pair of gigantic crossed swords at the nearby parade ground but didn't know how to get through the maze of fences. The massive hands holding the swords have netting attached to them full of helmets collected from the bodies of Iranian soldiers killed in the Iran/Iraq War. The Americans are keen to pull the swords down, in case they encourage support for the ex-dictator. In our attempt to get through the maze we got stuck in some mud but four-wheel drive eventually did the trick. I was half looking forward to asking Brendan to tie the camel, the two porcupines, 30 dogs and the cheetah to the front bumper like a scene out of a Walt Disney film but it never came to that. It was already 3pm and my flight out was scheduled for 3.45pm so popping a saddle on the cheetah might have been a superior option.

Then back to the increasingly familiar sight of long lines of cars waiting at US Army checkpoints, Iraqis with hands on their heads being jabbed with metal detectors, reminding me of the occupied West Bank: the humiliation, the lack of courtesy, the seemingly random and illogical conversations at the checkpoints. There is nothing like it to encourage resistance potentially leading to the vicious circles of violence so familiar elsewhere. Heyrick pointed out the folly of setting up permanent checkpoints like this, making them so vulnerable to attack. He contrasted it with the tactic employed in Northern Ireland of setting up a checkpoint in random places for a maximum of ten minutes at a time. Heyrick had slipped into the habit of driving around these queues and negotiating with the soldiers either having joined the front of the queue or having bolted down the military lane. This time the soldier told us we could pass but that an Iraqi pedestrian in the main queue was claiming to be attached to DHL at the airport. Sure enough Yahya came running towards us in his yellow DHL T-shirt. He had rushed home on hearing that his mother had fallen and broken her arm. There was such a commotion outside his house he worried something more serious had happened, but fortunately a broken arm was the extent of it and he accompanied her to the hospital in an ambulance before returning to work.

Back to the airport to discover that the plane had not yet arrived from Bahrain so I was not going to be leaving any time soon. In any case, I was in no hurry as long as the enchanting Yasmin was still in the DHL office. Heyrick dragged me away for a tour of the airport. First stop, the part under the control of the Australian contingent. Very polite, very professional, and here the questioning had a welcome thread of logic to it. We parked behind the old air navigation building and I waited in the car while Heyrick went in for his daily briefing. Or rather, I took this opportunity to relieve myself behind the jeep. I hadn't quite finished when Heyrick re-emerged from the building and started marching towards me. I thought the timing should just about work out and watched his approach over my shoulder through the windows of the car just in case I had to speed up, only to glance forward and discover a female Australian soldier parking her car right in front of me. I nodded an embarrassed apology to her and slipped back into the jeep. As we drove off she still seemed a long way from regaining her composure.

Regrettably the US marines had been let loose on the main terminal building and had caused major damage as well as laying turds everywhere - apparently not the first time they have played this trick on enemy property. It reminded me of the Israelis who smeared faeces around the Palestinian Ministry of Culture in 2002. Even the pavements outside the building were dotted with piles of lever arch files spewing official paperwork. Out of sight, behind the terminal building were the remains of the passenger jets in the distinctive greens of Iraqi Airways. The marines moved in and destroyed what was left of them after the airport had been taken. After the war the Iraqis may have turned to looting in a mad scramble after 12 years of sanctions but that surprises me less than the wanton destruction by the US troops for entertainment or maybe more sinister feelings towards the vanquished.

The night patrols are now perceived as being so dangerous that one GI spoke of how he would regularly vomit before climbing into his vehicle. By 6pm Wednesday the number of American soldiers killed by hostile fire since President Bush declared the end of the war stood at 89. Some checkpoints had been dismantled having become too dangerous to man. We drove past the open tents of the detainees to the west of the airport. My guess is the Iraqis in there have about as much chance of justice as detainees in communist China. I spent the rest of the afternoon in the DHL office studying, chatting to Yasmin and Zeinab and helping the latter to read the difficult handwriting on the address labels. It was Zeinab's first day. Yasmin was fielding requests for parcels she could not track because for one week the CIA had been using the frequency DHL had been allocated by the US military.

The pilot for the return journey shook my hand, took my jump seat permission and had started up the stairs to the plane when he swung around and shouted over the noise of the engines 'What did my father do to your mother I wonder?' I replied 'Just chatting to my friend Heyrick and will be up in a minute if that's alright with you' assuming my ears were playing tricks with me but it transpired his family name was Herbert too.

The plane's late arrival meant the race was on to get the containers loaded and take off before the sun set. Heyrick won't let DHL planes take off after sunset. As I 'calmly' surveyed the scene to judge for myself whether I would be forced to spend a night in Baghdad, I could only count the charming captain and myself ready to board. Yuri, the first officer, had fallen for Nuha, a half Egyptian half Iraqi employee of DHL based in Baghdad, and typically the two of them slip into the cockpit for some privacy during his hour-long stopovers at the airport. That the cockpit is the most comfortable place in the airport goes some of the way to explaining why Heyrick and team still go back downtown every evening to sleep despite the obvious danger. Yuri, Belgian of Eastern European extraction, met Nuha in June when, having flown the 16 consecutive days in his contract, he was asked to fly one more day to fill in for someone. God was clearly looking in his direction that day. We managed with about ten minutes of sunlight to go, though as the pilot was starting the engines, all three crew members chimed in with an 'Oh no! Let's get the fuck out of here'. I didn't dare ask what the problem was but agreed instantly. (An airplane had just requested permission to take off with one of its four engines down. The captain explained to me that, though possible, this was an extremely dangerous manoeuvre that involved using two engines to gain speed before engaging the third, thus avoiding putting too much stress on the chassis. Done badly it can cause the plane to flip over. If it catches fire, you die, if not you might escape with a few bruises.) As we made our steep ascent the sun was squinting at us from the horizon, and dark smoke was rising from the downtown area.

It was pitch black by the time Basra appeared, visible from a long way away thanks to five raging fires, each a spookily similar distance from the next. According to Captain Herbert the British forces had been putting them out only to have the arsonists light them again, so had resolved to leave them burning. The lights of Abadan were clearly visible across the border in Iran. Beyond Kuwait City we flew past the offshore rigs each marked out by a small flame.

Bahrain air traffic control had us doing loops to buy time for the slower aircraft in front of us so we got a good look at Dahran/Dammam/Khobar and the causeway connecting them to Bahrain. Though not visible in its entirety, the causeway was identifiable by a collection of lights at its centre marking the customs post. I joked that funding for the causeway must have taken all of about ten seconds, judging by the enthusiasm with which Saudis bolt across it on a Thursday afternoon (the start of the Gulf weekend) to get a drink and time with the glamour models but the South African flight engineer had heard that there had been considerable resistance to it from Bahrainis. It seems they ultimately worked out which side their bread is buttered on. Having landed on Al Muharraq, air traffic control made us wait between the two main runways. A Gulf Air plane landed in front of us and Captain Herbert recognised the pilot's voice as being that of an ex-colleague from Sabena. Then who should appear but the Moldovans in the Antonov, to our cheers and a raft of imitation Russian accents. We flashed our headlights a few times to remind the control tower we were still sitting there: the crew was dead keen to get to the hotel buffet and knock back a few beers and Captain Herbert was looking forward to surprising his ex-colleague. Reunited with the Russians back from Bagram, the day had taken me a full circle.

My first glimpse of Iraq, a country I have dreamed of visiting for more than a decade, was a depressing experience despite the excitement. It was reassuring to spot traits common to other parts of the ex-Ottoman empire like the way the police direct traffic and the grunt the civil servants make down the telephone to acknowledge tit-bits of information from their juniors. The Iraqis reacted positively to a foreigner speaking Arabic as soon as the initial surprise had passed. I struggle to find an analogy but when I opened my mouth it must have been akin to finding a Native American speaking with a broad Liverpudlian accent. As well as being associated with films, the Egyptian accent is also the language of comedy so even saying something deadly serious would regularly elicit a smile before a serious response, in the way an Irish accent sometimes makes the English smile. Hearing the Iraqis speak tickled me in that almost all the vocabulary comes from modern standard Arabic, the mother ship, which is fairly uniform across the Arab World, but until you are familiar with a dialect you cannot predict which word they will use, nor where the tonal inflections will occur. Everyone I asked said they were pleased Saddam Hussein was gone but clearly they were disappointed by the lack of security, the state of the economy and that their borders were still open to unsavoury types chased out of their previous havens by America's war on terror. The people I spoke to didn't really have a view on the US and UK governments deceiving their people into declaring war, nor would you if you had never experienced democracy, but they were very disappointed that a responsibility as great as the lives of more than 25m people had been taken on with so little advanced planning. The most obvious frustration seemed to be the humiliation at the checkpoints and the house-to-house searches based on questionable intelligence. I'm already impatient to return.

APPENDIX

'Gunfire rattled through the streets of downtown Baghdad earlier Wednesday morning after about 1,000 protesters stormed a police station near the Palestine Hotel, where many foreign journalists are based, to demand jobs with the Iraqi police force.

'Many complained they had paid bribes to have their names added to the recruitment list but had not been hired. After protesters set two cars ablaze, police opened fire, sending demonstrators, motorists and pedestrians scurrying for cover.

'At least one policeman was seen firing his pistol directly into the crowd; witnesses said two people were injured. Police Captain Hashim Habib Mohsen said some of the demonstrators fired on police.'

Source: Agencies (on the Internet)

15 FEEDBACK

Inviting 360 degree feedback from staff provides an invaluable insight into the way a business really works. It leads to a deepening of relationships within the organizations, an understanding of issues and obstacles, and the promise of evergreen improvement.

(The Encyclopedia of Current Business Orthodoxy)

AN IRAQI'S STORY:

'My name is Zaid, the youngest after one brother and one sister among our small family. My father, a doctor is a pediatrician here in Iraq, having got his diploma in child health and FRCP from London University and Glasgow University in the early sixties. My mother is half Lebanese (from her father) half Iraqi (from her mother). She has a higher degree in English literature and in teaching English with a foreign language from England too. My older brother is a mechanical engineer who lives in Australia now and my older sister is an architect who is getting her masters now in the Jordanian university.

I was born November 9th 1980 in Baghdad in a private hospital where the electricity was off because of an air raid in the early days of the Iraqi-Iranian war, which was not a sign of optimism for a happy peaceful life. A year later my father had the good fortune to be invited to spend a year conducting research as a visiting professor in Georgetown University in Washington DC. It was especially lucky because the government (Saddam of course) had already stopped travelling completely by any means except for official business of the government itself and a few other minor exceptions. So we all spent the year with him living in Maryland where both my brother and sister completed a school year (primary school for my sister and high school for my brother). It was a tough year for my brother. He said it required a massive adjustment and the odd fist fight before he felt he fit in and could make any friends. He always advises me to stand up for myself in any foreign society if I travel for work or study because it is always a hard start. He and my sister passed that year with good grades and were all able to feel settled. The only thing I got was asthma, aggravated by the tree pollens and the snowy winter. I ended up spending a lot of time in the hospital, including Christmas Day and New Year's Eve. At the end of that year my father turned down the chance to stay on, much to our regret, and brought us back here to Iraq. His cause was simply that his parents back here were getting older and needed more and more medical attention. Being the eldest son and a doctor, he felt he had to come back to look after them.

My earliest memories date from when I was four and five years old back in Baghdad. I did not go to kindergarten because of my repeated asthma attack and my need for the inhaler. I could not run or play football with other children much (football is the number one sport in Iraq) and I became introverted in my first year and struggled to make friends. But it wasn't all bad and my memories of that period are warmer for not being scarred by the exhaustion of war. All I could remember were a few brief air raids by the Iranian Air Force, which was pretty inexpert and easily hunted down by our Russian supplied SAM missiles and air defences. The real war was being fought on the distant front lines, where young men were being killed every day in the hundreds and thousands. From month to month they came back to their parents and young wives or to a child they have never seen. Most households suffered losses. I was lucky that our family and relatives did not have anyone in the military so I did not appreciate how grave the losses were at the time. All these men lost their life in what they thought was a battle to defend their country's honour and their home. After the end of the war it slowly became clear that it had been nothing but a chess game for Saddam.

I remember clearly a particularly bad time when our cities were being bombarded by long range missiles. They used to fall anytime and anywhere, wiping out a few houses and terrifying an area of the city. Iran did not have satellite guiding systems or precision targeting mechanisms so there was never any way of determining where they might fall. They were just sent in the general direction of Baghdad. One of them fell on a crowded primary school for children in the middle of the day, massacring the children. Another one fell on a crowded market area when my mother and I were nearby and we were almost knocked down to the ground by the blast wave. Things took a turn for the better once Saddam had been provided with chemical weapons by the U.S. and began to use them on the front line. He quickly got the upper hand and we could sense the approach of victory. Peace was finally declared in August 1988.

I remember we used to call him Uncle Saddam as children

and we were forced to love him and sing songs about him every morning, with his pictures and copies of his speeches plastered around the school. We had one national T.V. channel and that was it. We did not have to use a remote control because there was no other channel to switch it to. It used to show battle news (without mentioning the losses) and play patriotic songs all the time. There was a 30 minute cartoon for children in the afternoon and one episode daily of an Arabic T.V. service that was followed by an old Arabic or American movie at night with the end of transmission at 12 o'clock. My mouth dropped in awe and wonder when I was told that in America or Europe there are 40 to 50 channels and that some of them are specialised for children and cartoons. We had two amusement parks only with primitive game equipments built in the early 70s. There was a single rickety rollercoaster, some overrun gardens and grimy restaurants. The park also had a small and neglected zoo, the destination for countless school trips (two or three times a year) or any family outing. There wasn't much else on offer, besides the dreary Natural History Museum. There was also a cinema for children showing some ancient cartoons but no one really enjoyed watching them. Fun for a child was very limited and simple and primitive, even in the capital and it must have been worse in the smaller towns and rural areas. When I saw pictures of myself as a one or two year old in Disney Land I looked at them as if I was on a different planet.

After the Iranian war we were blessed with a single prosperous year filled with the unfamiliar sensation of hope and optimism. We were reconnected to the outside world again. There was a McDonalds, new cars were imported and different agencies and trademarks shops. Travelling was also allowed and we booked a holiday to Paris for two weeks. Then in one dark night, out of the blue, it was all turned upside down with Saddam's famous move of invading Kuwait. The night before the invasion he made a stupid precautionary measure, giving a general alarm for the evacuation of Baghdad for a few days because of a nuclear threat of Israel. We did not understand what the hell was going on but it was only a matter of hours before we heard on the radio that the Iraqi army was in control of all of Kuwait. We were stunned. Nobody knew what lay behind the decision to attack and there had been no preparatory explanation. Everyone knows what followed and the scale of the embargo that followed and of course the Gulf War (Desert Storm). Those were really some black days - black years - in which the deepest suffering was felt by the ordinary people. We lacked food, basic items (sugar, rice, wheat); there were no more sweets and ice cream and essential drugs in hospitals. Men, women and children were dying because of the lack of simple drugs and vaccines. It felt as if we had been cast back into the middle ages, with the complete destruction of the infrastructure (water supply, electricity). The uprising in the south that followed the war was brutally squashed. Only recently has the full extent of the horrors and the cost to human lives been clear. The early nineties were the toughest. Services were slow to return and the embargo designed to weaken Saddam only succeeded in making our lives a living hell.

At the time I was in intermediate school which comes between primary and high school. That's when boys and girls are split apart, not to rejoin until they go to college. These were grey years because the teenagers here have nothing to do - certainly not the wild fun parties or sex their American counterparts are beginning to enjoy. Boys who want to get a girlfriend have to skip school and go to the girls school in the hope of being able to find someone willing to take their phone number so they can be a boyfriend and girlfriend. And if he is lucky he can meet her secretly somewhere. Even then it usually doesn't go beyond first base and even more rarely second base. So the closest you get to sex as a teenager is a worn out magazine or a tape. But besides these frustrations, it is a pretty simple age. There is no responsibility beyond getting good results at school. We used to enjoy the simplest things - hanging out on our bikes or playing video games. I made some of my best friends back then and many of them remain close to me today. We also used to enjoy smoking a discreet cigarette at every chance. Maybe one of the good things about isolation from the world was the absence of any addictive drugs or marijuana or anything. The naughtiest thing you could do was to drink some beer and there weren't really any bars. The absence of copyright regulations for any multimedia, entertainment or software product also worked in our favour. I became a big fan of American and English music (pop at first) at the upsurge of band fever (Backstreet Boys, Five, Spice Girls and N Sync) because album copies were cheap and easy to get. Celine Dion and many more. The latest movies were also easily available in pirate copy (Titanic, Mission Impossible, Scram.......) within a month of their release from the US. In the same way you could get any software from Windows to Autocard to Adobe Photoshop latest release for $1.

So when we wanted to hang out and have fun in the weekend or something like a holiday we could only go to a restaurant and rent a movie to watch at home afterwards and have a barbecued kebab afterwards in the garden with friends. Later there were places where you could go to play billiards or playstation but there certainly weren't any malls or supermarkets to hang around.

On the river (by the Tigris) there are lots of coffee shops, simple, oriental, some of them built in the 20th century where people of all ages go to have tea (the national drink) and smoke the hubble bubble whilst playing dominos or checkers or chess. There are also some beautiful little restaurants serving delicious fish brought daily fresh by the local river fisherman and kept in water until you choose the one you want to grill. (NOTE. We saw these in an old bath tub at the Sheraton Hotel. They had been caught in the Tigris, the same river that acts as the sewer for Baghdad).

The final year in high school is usually a very tough year because it decides your future and which college you are going to go to. The end of year final exam is set by the Ministry of Education, not the school itself, and is the same for the whole country. Usually, everyone aims to study medicine, dentistry or pharmacology. If they don't manage to qualify for them then further down the list are economics or business administration. Maybe this explains our disastrous economy and financial system. Education is totally free in Iraq and that is one of the great accomplishments of the country early in its independence from the British. Saddam, as part of his programmed destruction, began to destroy this system by giving the teachers low salaries that were not enough for a day, forcing them to depend on giving some private lectures for the able students in the afternoons to make a living. It reached a level where students were almost entirely dependent on private lectures in all subjects, especially in that critical final year. Those families that could not pay for their sons suffered. In universities the problem was even greater and it caused the immigration of some of the greatest scientific minds in the country with Phds from Oxford or Harvard, with years of experience leaving the acute to suffer. This affected the future of the young in the country. I was fortunate to be accepted in the college of medicine in Baghdad University.

The practice of medicine is one of the best in the region. The first college of medicine (in the modern meaning of practice) was established in 1927 with an English Dean and mixed Iraqi and English staff. So the teaching of medicine was based on and linked with the English schools of medicine which produced some skilled doctors in Iraq over the years. But this solid medical institution was one of the first to be affected by the embargo, contributing to an already exhausted health care system. I started to learn this from my first year in medical college. Our college provides text books for example. The latest one we had was of 1985 edition which forced us to buy copies from local print shops with low quality black and white paper. The anatomy lab had one cadaver to dissect by all of the 200 student class each year (ironic under Saddam's rule of death). The shortage of basic drugs in the hospitals lead to high infant mortality rates (93.2/1000 compared to about 7.1/1000 for USA). But still Iraqi people are hard working and enthusiastic to do their job whatever it is and that kept life going under these distressing burdens, from the student to the doctor, from the engineer to the builder. They all learned to work with what was available and not to complain because it would be of no use and sometimes resulted in being sent for execution.

So back to life in college here. Boys and girls get to be mixed again in an educational environment. But at this age and in this strict society it is not for relationships and going steady and sharing accommodation and boyfriend/girlfriend type of life. It is only for seeking your life mate so those that like each other try to get to know each other better within the college environment. Then they get engaged to have more privacy, which could last from months to years. If after all that they find that they fit each other and love each other it ends up in marriage, usually just after graduation. Marriage of course is getting harder and harder financially because of the desperate state of the economy and the difficulties young graduates have in affording their own place or a car. So in most cases they will end up living with their parents after getting their own room in the house if it has enough or adding some rooms to it if it was tight. This resulted in many people emigrating to look for work and a better situation. The only loser was the country whose professional classes were shattered (either by migration or by being persecuted). College life produced some beautiful friendships with groups of boys and girls hanging out and talking labs or clinical sessions together all the time. You become close friends and support each other in everything from clinical sessions to birthday parties or go to lunch together or go to a club and some of these groups remain for life even after getting married and becoming family groups.

For the time being I am at my final year in college and now Saddam is captured and the war (freedom for Iraq), at least the major military phase, was ended with the fall of the statue in April. But still I am writing these lines by candle light due to the lack of electricity (and that is after eight months of the coalition administration of Iraq and the horror that we survived during the war) and after it with the shooting and insecurity. Terrorism has stolen the happiness of the fall of Saddam and his regime (when he was in power no Iraqi would have dared to write these pages and describe the suffering even if I was to keep it in my own desk). But none of the coalition promises have yet been realized and many aspects are even worse. The people of Iraq have not even enjoyed the taste of freedom because of the suffocating shortage of basic services and supplies and even money from salaries. But the people of Iraq, who never imagined the reign of fear would end (they expected him to pass power onto his family) still have hope that this is a transitional period and that tomorrow will bring these simple dreams of living a peaceful and secure life for them and for their children. The irony is that they are currently one of the poorest people in the world whilst they are living on one of the richest lands in the world. We are rich with the black gold, a blessing and a curse of this nation. So who knows what this country is going to see in its next chapter.

16 RISK MANAGEMENT

Unexpected developments are a constant feature of business life. Contingency planning is the most effective way of managing the risks they present. This requires a detailed exploration of possible scenarios and consideration of how best to prepare for these possible eventualities.

(The Encyclopedia of Current Business Orthodoxy)

DHL continued to flourish, increasing the numbers of aircraft and people in the country. In an effort to spread the DHL gospel we cooked a barbecue for the Australian Air Force, who ran the control tower at the airport. It was a rather surreal experience sitting on the roof as the artillery shells were being fired from one side of the airport over our heads at some of the bad guys on the other side. These attempts to silence the enemy around the airport had some success but did not prevent us forming the DHL Iraq aerobatic club, with our planes doing some very exciting flying to keep any potential bad guys guessing. The European pilots relished the opportunity to fly out to Iraq where there were few restrictions and they had the chance to push the planes to the limit, resulting in some very entertaining photos, especially when I had the chance to sit in the cockpit. At times they did get a little carried away and one of the Airbus had three punctures following rather a heavy landing. I had never worked with aircraft before but soon discovered that when they go wrong they do so in style and it took three days to change the wheels and sort out the punctures.

The Antonov crew members had been behaving themselves and I was due to do a proving flight to Fallujah, a well known hot spot. However, the flight to Fallujah met with delays as a US helicopter was shot down and all on board were killed. It was a tragedy made all the more poignant by the fact that they were flying out to go on some well deserved leave. Among the dead were a couple of soldiers that had worked in the hangar next to the office. For the next week or so the soldiers were not their ebullient selves. It was the first of their group that had been killed since the end of hostilities. It happened just as I was due to go on leave and I couldn't help feeling a pang of guilt as I headed back to the UK for my engagement party. The party was a fantastic collection of old friends but it felt strange having been sat in Baghdad only twenty four hours previously. It really hit me how different my life had become. It seemed quite odd to be standing in front of a sea of faces regaling them with stories of crazy Antonov pilots. I couldn't help wondering about all the staff, ex-pats and Iraqis and hoping that they were safe. Here I was in the middle of London a million miles away from the crackle of gunfire and occasional explosion that I would often be hearing at this time of night.

To most people at home Saturday 22nd November was the day England won the rugby world cup. For me it was the day my one real fear in Iraq was realized. As usual I awoke to the sound of the generator spluttering into life. The burning question that needed to be answered was how I was going to find a TV in Baghdad that was going to be showing the rugby final. I soon realized that I only had one option, assuming I made it back in time from a flying visit to Mosul. That was to go up to the control tower, into enemy territory, and watch the match with the Australian Air Force.

The day was as normal as ever and started with a mini drama. The hand brake was left off a truck that rolled in slow motion towards the Antonov. I could already imagine the call to head office, 'hello, can you send out a new left wing please, the old one has a truck embedded in it.' Fortunately Super-Rad, as Rado is now called, was fleet of foot and managed to launch his 180kg frame at the offending truck and stop it dead in its tracks.

Meanwhile the Airbus arrived from Bahrain and I went up to the cockpit to talk to the crew and have a morning croissant and coffee with them. The chat was jovial. It was the captain's last flight for a couple of weeks as he was due to return home for a fortnight's leave. In fact he had been due to fly back to Brussels that morning but there had been a mix up with the aircraft crews and so he had volunteered for an early flight into Baghdad. I bade him farewell, wished him a Happy Christmas and a safe flight back to Bahrain.

The plane taxied down the runway, I finished gathering my things for the flight to Mosul and wandered out onto the pan to watch the airbus take off. The pilots had been doing some spectacular flying over the past six months. It is not often that an Airbus is able to take off on the first quarter of the runway and then perform a steep bank past the tower before it heads away on its journey home. The plane disappeared into the clear blue sky in the distance. I was about to board the Antonov when a huge cloud of smoke billowed from the disappearing Airbus. Immediately, the Airbus began to lose height with smoke streaming from the left wing. I was praying that it was only some sort of engine failure but deep down knew that my worst fear was realized. It had been hit by a missile. I rang the tower to find out if they could speak to the pilots and see what had happened. As we spoke I watched in horror as a flame shot out of the wing. Eric, the captain, could see nothing but explained that he heard a huge bang and lost all hydraulics. To the uninitiated this means he was unable to use his wing flaps, tail flaps or ultimately his brakes. Try and imagine that you are driving down the motorway in the fast lane and your steering wheel and brakes fail. But you have some capacity to steer because you have two accelerators that control your wheels on either side of the car. If this is not difficult enough add vertical movement into the equation.

Whilst watching, I could clearly see that he was struggling to control the aircraft and was trying to lose height but was doing this more rapidly than intended. Thankfully he leveled out and as he did a huge flame shot down the length of the aircraft as the fuel tank at the end of the wing ignited. A feeling of dread swept through my body as images of the Columbia space shuttle and the Air France Concorde flashed through my mind, but by a miracle the fuel caused no further explosion. For the next twenty minutes the plane limped around in a circuit, getting lower and lower as Eric used the power of first one engine and then the other to steer the plane in a downwards spiral. My mind was racing but the events felt like a very drawn out car crash and seemed to be happening in slow motion. I was desperately trying to think of a way I could help. But actually the only things to be done were to ensure all the emergency services were ready and to make sure Head Office knew what was going on so that they did not get caught unawares by any reporters. I also made sure the employees were calmed down as the Iraqis were working themselves into a frenzy and this merely acted as a catalyst, cranking up the tension. My concern was that this would cause someone on the ground to do something irrational and we could then have two problems on our hands. I kept one eye on the plane and the other on the staff, particularly the Iraqis.

After what felt like a month the crew managed to bring the plane back towards the airport and now they were going to be faced with the task of landing a plane with no brakes or flaps. It was clear that Eric was going for the military side of the airport. There were less obstacles near the runway. At this point all the Iraqis rushed towards the vehicles as they had clearly decided they were going to drive to the other side of the airport to watch the landing. I made them get out and handed all the keys to one of the ex-pats. The last thing we needed was forty hysterical staff driving round the airport at break neck speed and then adding to the drama of the scene on their arrival.

I jumped into the jeep and drove round to be there for Eric's landing. The plane was veering from one side to the other as he tried to straighten her on the approach. He was going far too fast and was still a good 50ft high over the first quarter of the runway. He cut the engines and the aircraft dropped out of the sky and landed with a crash and a billow of smoke and dust. By reverse thrusting the engines he was able to slow the plane a little but then he slewed towards the parked helicopters, overcompensated and went off the other side of the runway. The Airbus hit the sand, which was like a fine powder and this not only slowed them down but also helped put out the flames that were still pouring from the wing.

I sped down the runway and watched the escape slides pop out of the exits. There was none of the orderly removal of shoes and crossing of arms that you see on the aircraft manuals. These guys were running down the escape slides as they evacuated. At the same time emergency crews, who had arrived almost instantaneously, started spraying the wing. Before they knew it, Eric, Steve and Mario were surrounded by the fire crew who were congratulating them and already the crowds were starting to come across the runway. They started to show the classic symptoms of shock. Steve and Mario were like stunned rabbits and Eric was dancing with joy, high on adrenalin. I pushed through the crowd embracing all three of them at once. I led them away from the rapidly expanding throng. The initial comments from Eric and Mario were 'the bastards shot us down' and Steve just said 'I'm 29 years old and I've just used up all my luck'. We took them to the car and over to the hospital. Here they underwent preliminary checks and all seemed physically fine. Eric meanwhile was now almost delirious and was dancing about outside, smoking and asking for women and whiskey. Rather than let them settle down we headed back to the plane as they needed to ensure they completed the close down procedures and picked up their documents and personal effects. More importantly there was also time to inspect the damage and they posed for photos. On returning to the plane the military had cordoned the area off and as soon as my phone rang I was glad they had reacted so quickly. CNN were hot on the trail then NBC, both of which I swiftly hung up on telling the latter that they had the wrong number. CNN then called again so I changed tactics realizing the wrong number gag wouldn't work and berated them for not paying their invoice for which they were two weeks late and this seemed to silence them. (Someone came to the DHL office two days later and paid it in full.)

This was the first time I really stopped to look at the plane. Originally white, it was covered in earth and sand. The left wing had a five foot hole about three quarters of the way along it and the fire crew were busy patching up a fuel leak with masking tape. Several of the tyres had burst under the impact of landing and razor wire and fencing was wrapped around the landing gear. The long, silver escape slides hung out of the sides. Up in the cockpit there was dust everywhere and anything that was not fixed had been thrown forward. The freight, however, had not moved due to the fact that there was only about five tonnes on board and all of the floor locks had done their job and held it in place.

By now the crew were looking a little worse for wear and having made calls home we headed off to the protection of the US Air Force compound. This enabled us to keep some distance from the press who were now on the airport and were frantically searching for the crew. The Military were superb and if I could pick a place to have a plane crash Baghdad would have been it. My priority now was damage limitation. I was in the enviable position of being cut off from the press but I really needed to get the pilots back to Bahrain. The last thing I wanted to do was to have to negotiate another of our aircraft in so that we could fly them out. Within an hour we managed to get the crew booked onto a USAF and an RAF flight. At least two helicopters and the RAF had been in the air watching the drama unfold and have since officially declared Eric a legend. They were all itching to get him onto their plane out so that he could talk them through every detail.

Prior to departure we had a rather surreal picnic in the

sun and within a couple of hours had them on a plane out of Baghdad. My next thought was to cover the hole up in the wing to prevent the photos being broadcast around the world. It was now dark and so the next morning, I got hold of a huge tarpaulin and two of us shuffled along the wing to cover the hole. Ironically it ended up being wrapped around the wing like a huge plaster, but this plane was not going to be getting better. The inevitable calls started coming through from DHL headquarters in Brussels and I repeated the events several dozen times. If this was to happen again I would be tempted to have someone to do this for me as I ended up spending an unnecessary amount of the time on the phone when I could have been organising other things.

The next job was to tow the aircraft out of the sand and back onto the runway. With the promise of pizza and KFC we were able to persuade a man with a large tractor to drag the plane backwards out of the sand. It was then pulled around to the aircraft graveyard where it settled in amongst all the Iraqi Airways planes that had been destroyed during the war. Post war the score now stood at 1-0 to Iraq. We also needed to retrieve the black boxes for the voice and instrument recordings. Having scrambled around looking for a black box 'somewhere in the back belly of the plane' and found nothing I left it to the professionals. Within 30 seconds they appeared with two large, bright orange oblong containers about the size of five four-packs of beer stacked on top of each other. I had ruled them out straight away because they were orange and oblong. No wonder we needed to leave it to the experts.

So an eventful couple of days, followed by a pregnant pause whilst more planes were organised to take the place of the carrier we had been using. We also found ourselves doing a bit more driving as we had to switch our international gateway to another airfield. It was whilst out and about that it dawned on me how many Iraqis have served in the army. The weather had got colder and wet and almost everyone seemed to be wearing green military jackets. If I was a member of the Coalition Forces it would have concerned me a great deal. Couple it with the killing of 50 'insurgents' in Samarra in December, each of whom had family and friends to galvanise into action, and there was no getting away from the scale of the task facing the coalition forces. This was encapsulated in the official security update that was issued to NGOs and civilian contractors.

NGO AND CIVILIAN CONTRACTORS BRIEF: 9 Dec 2003

Summary of Recent Security Events:
1. The following significant incidents took place during the reporting period:

   a. **22 Nov 03:** A convoy of empty cargo trucks travelling from BAGHDAD to KUWAIT was hijacked north of NASARIYAH on route TAMPA. One person was shot and wounded.

   b. **4 Dec 03:** A blue people carrier vehicle arrived at SAFWAN IZP station. The occupants stated that three armed men in white Caprice had attempted to hijack their vehicle and that the back window of their car had been shot out. The hijacking attempt took place at the junction of Routes MAUI and TOPEKA. The white caprice was last seen heading north towards AZ ZUBAYR.

2. In the past, types of attack have varied from stoning, and the climbing on to the back of moving trucks in order to steal food by throwing it overboard, through to armed robbery, hijacking and murder. Direct attacks on vehicles are now becoming more widespread. The reasons for the targeting remain crime related, for the cargo being carried or the vehicles and parts. The perpetrators are likely to be opportunistic thieves or organised criminal gangs.

3. Over recent months, the majority of the attacks reported in the Multinational Division (South East) (MND (SE)) area of operations have been in the BASRA / NASARIYA / SAFWAN triangle and along Main Supply Routes (MSRs) TAMPA and JACKSON. These attacks are of great concern not only to the aid agencies but also to the Coalition Forces. Reporting suggests that Kuwaiti registered vehicles in particular are targeted. Other threats include sabotage by both criminal, Former Regime Elements (FRE) and attacks on civilian vehicles. In the light of the attack on the UN building in BAGHDAD, fixed locations such as the CPA building in BASRA remain an area of vulnerability and there is concern that terrorist elements may focus on these as 'soft targets'.

Current Threats:
4. **Civilian Vehicles.** The standard 4x4 off-road type vehicles used by both the military and other western agencies are now well recognised as potentially softer targets and are therefore vulnerable. The reporting of vehicle hijackings of civilian and contractors'

vehicles seem to be steadily increasing. NGO vehicles will always be perceived as being a 'soft target' by criminal elements due to their limited protection from attack. Trucks are particularly vulnerable to attack when they breakdown or sustain punctures as other vehicles in the convoy are not permitted to stop to give assistance. There have been incidents in the past of convoys being forced to stop or slow down due to spikes and rocks placed in the road. Hijacked vehicles are either sold on complete or, broken down for spare parts. Both options are lucrative for the perpetrators and stolen vehicles are very often dispatched over Iraq's relatively porous borders.

5. **Personnel.** Recent reporting has also suggested that the drivers are being bribed, by criminal elements, to drive to meeting points to hand the trucks and cargos over and report them as being hijacked. The drivers can earn several hundred dollars for this, significantly more that their legitimate wages. Reporting from Baghdad suggests that vehicle 'chop shops' are on the increase, and theft of civilian cars is back up to five to eight per day.

6. **Locally Employed Civilians.** It is recognised and accepted that the more NGOs become established throughout Iraq, and humanitarian aid programs progress, there will be a greater need for the use of local labour. There are general concerns about the possibility of this situation being exploited by FREs or criminals. In particular, FREs may see this as an opportunity to get closer access to coalition

force (CF) locations and personnel, with a view to gathering intelligence, due to the close links between NGOs and CF. Care must be taken when employing local civilians, and some degree of screening must be conducted before employment. In such cases, this issuing of identity cards must be addressed and is the responsibility of the local employer/contractor.

7. There have been recent reports of threats against any civilian who works with, for or assists the CF, and therefore NGOs must be included in this category. The form such an attack would take is unknown. Attacks and demonstrations continue against CF, especially against US forces in their sector, and therefore the possibility exists of an aid convoy being inadvertently involved in such AO. The attacks against military convoys have steadily been improving in relation to their *Modus Operandi*, and they have been increasingly sophisticated. Recent attacks in northern Iraq have seen coordinated small-arms, improvised explosive devices (IEDs) and rocket propelled grenade assaults, showing a degree of command and control within anti-CF elements. Clearly such attacks are very rare in the MND (SE) AO and there have been none conducted against NGOs and other civilian organisations.

Assessment:
8. It is assessed that the primary reason for hostile action against NGOs and civilian contractors is simply to acquire their vehicles and/or cargo. There will

always be some degree of anti-western sentiment throughout Iraq, which may manifest itself as violent acts towards some NGOs, but to date this has been minimal. Serious threats to life will likely be in the form of Vehicle Borne IEDs (VBIEDs), such as the two already directed against the UN in BAGHDAD, high-profile static targets.

9. It is assessed that the coordinated attacks, already seen against military targets, may not be used against NGO convoys or transiting vehicles. Some reporting suggests that such anti-NGO activity could further isolate the groups conducting such acts, as the vast majority of the population realise the benefits such organisations bring to the rebuilding of Iraq and its infrastructure.

Recommendations:
10. **Security Measures and Travel Advice.** The threat exists both during the day and at night, but currently the most dangerous times for travel, those seeing the most anti-CF activity, is between 2000 hrs and 0100 hrs. *It would therefore be advisable to conduct all movement of humanitarian aid using a minimum of two vehicles and during daylight hours.*

11. It is also advised that aid workers remain as anonymous as possible within their area of residence. Since most of the attacks have taken place on MSR TAMPA and MAUI within the BASRA / NASIRIYA / SAFWAN triangle it is advisable to take extra care when in this area. The murder of a CPA guarding employee

highlights the need to remind all personnel of the following precautions when travelling in vehicles:

a. If issued with protective clothing, wear it at all times.
b. Restrict your movements to essential journeys only.
c. If travelling with armed personnel, ensure that weapons are visible.
d. Civilian vehicles are vulnerable, particularly when stationary and moving slowly.
e. Be aware that children have been used in order to slow target vehicles down.
f. Vary your routes and avoid fixed patterns and timings.
g. All movements by road must contain a minimum of two vehicles.
h. Do not become isolated.
i. If unfamiliar with your route, take a local guide or colleague who has good local knowledge. Make sure each vehicle contains adequate mapping for the entire route.
j. Beware of local driving standards.

12. **Guidelines in the event of a suspected IED**. No advice can possibly cover every eventuality in the event of the discovery of an IED. IEDs have been known to be hidden by the side of the road in piles of rubbish, old tyres, culverts, and trees or suspended from lamp posts. Obstacles have also been placed on roads to channel traffic in to a 'kill zone.' In general terms, if an IED is suspected, the following action should be taken:

a. Confirm and report location and description of suspect device to MND(SE).

b. Maintain a safe distance of at least 100m, using hard cover if possible. Warn others to stay clear of the area.

c. If in doubt, turn your vehicle around and seek an alternative route.

Conclusion

13. Recent trends continue to indicate a heightened interest in the acquisition by hostile groups and criminal gangs, of civilian and contractors' vehicles. Therefore the greatest threats to NGOs exist when they are travelling. Other threats include those from FRE groups who seek to disrupt the reparatory work that is being carried out. The dangers faced by NGOs within Southern Iraq remain serious and all due care must be taken, particularly when in transit. Attackers, criminal or otherwise, are encouraged by the relative isolation and vulnerability of NGOs and the value of their cargos. Certain elements are carrying out attacks purely to disrupt the efforts of aid agencies to reduce the country to normality.

14. Whilst attacks on convoys have been well documented, it is assessed that small vehicle moves are most vulnerable. Advice is therefore given to confine small vehicle moves to essential journeys and to exercise all due care, especially around the BASRA / NASIRIYA / SAFWAN triangle and along MSRs TAMPA, MAUI and JACKSON.

15. The threat of attacks against high-profile static locations, by such methods as VBIEDs, remains throughout the AO. This threat, however, can be countered by the use of sterile zones outside such locations, the vigilance of staff and thorough searching of vehicles before being allowed access to secure compounds.

End of report

17 STRESS

Stress is an inevitable feature of modern working life. The performance imperative places considerable pressure on employees at every level and they react in a wide variety of ways. It is important to be sensitive to the subtleties of their pyschology and respect their emotional idiosyncrasies.

(The Encyclopedia of Current Business Orthodoxy)

There were some extremely strange people working out there. I would like to think that I was at the less strange end of the spectrum but the fact that I was there does leave me open to various calls of weirdness. Every now and then I had a reality check and realised that although I had become used to my surroundings the environment was far from normal. It was the little things that I tended to treat as part of every day life. I liked to try and squeeze a run in at the airport at some point in the morning as running in Baghdad wasn't an option. At the airport I could stretch my legs and get some time away from everything - that was until a Black Hawk or an Apache helicopter disturbed my reverie as they buzzed over head or I ventured near the runway as the planes came and went. I could never get over the feeling that it would be regarded as extremely odd to go for a jog on Heathrow airport yet out there it had become a way of life. We were fed and watered by Uncle Sam in the various dining facilities, or D Facs as they were known. These varied in quality; The Bob Hope on BIAP fed 3000 per sitting and was housed within a huge rigid tent, which was about the size of an aircraft hangar. The food was of reasonable quality except for the ice cream which they took very seriously and was excellent! Downsides? Only that with half the tent as a kitchen the smell of chip fat remained with you all day. As a result, I was constantly on the hunt for a new venue and occasionally found myself donning body armour to go to another base purely because their D Fac had fresh bread.

There was a tremendous mix of personalities there - Indians who had been shipped in as chefs and cleaners, Malays who were electricians and plumbers, Nepalese and Fijians who tended to do the security roles. The Nepalese were all former British army Gurkhas and were there to top up their army pension and also because they were fleeing the deteriorating situation in Nepal. The Maoists are beginning to gain a stronger foothold in Nepal and they have a habit of kidnapping former Gurkhas and forcing them to train the Maoist insurgents. Any sign of resistance results in the individual and his family being killed, so why hang around when you can save your skin and earn a few dollars in the process? The Fijians were also there in pursuit of the dollar and this, combined with the British Army's recruiting drive for Fijians, has decimated their Army and Police Force. They were an imposing bunch and were constantly challenging us to a game of rugby. With a handful of former internationals and the rest all very large we found it easy to make excuses and blame the priority of work.

All societies and cultures are full of contradictions but the US Military is positively overflowing. On the one hand there was the cheese factor that came to the fore, exemplified when people put messages at the bottom of emails: 'I can do all things through Christ which strengthens me. The road to success is not straight. There is a curve called Failure, a loop called Confusion, speed bumps called Friends, red lights called Enemies, caution lights called Family. You will have flats called Jobs. But, if you have a spare called Determination, an engine called Perseverance, insurance called Faith, a driver called Jesus, you will make it to a place called Success.' Admirable sentiments, but then on the other hand, I would hear that some GIs had got hold of a puppy at the Zoo and fed it to the lions. It was so tempting to generalize but for an organisation that is so ethnically diverse, the US Army are surprisingly racist. Unless you are Black, White, Hispanic or Oriental you are politely referred to as a TCN (Third Country National). A prime example of their paranoia was a weekly occurrence with a company based in a camp within the CPA, near our office. They employed Indians to clean and maintain the porta-cabin villages that had been erected. Once a week they had to close down their operation for the morning as the K9 (play on the word Canine) unit sent the sniffer dogs through looking for explosives. Obviously K9 found nothing, but the searches continued because as far as they were concerned they were dealing with Iraqis. I had heard from our office in Mosul that this paranoia led to the military accidentally shooting an Iraqi at the front gate of the camp. When I asked for more details they said that he had been shot 14 times and was then taken into hospital. Although they were under threat this was ridiculous. Another example of soldiers behaving crassly occurred in Mosul when they set dogs loose on the shooting range and shot them. Soldiers throughout the world are ill disciplined but this kind of behaviour also stemmed from boredom, lack of leadership from their superiors and poor training. There were 140,000 troops out there, a third of whom carried no ammunition and therefore didn't even venture outside camp. This boredom stemmed from the 'lets throw money at the problem' approach to soldiering. The amount of money spent on the military operation was mind-boggling. For example there was a changeover of troops that began in December. The UK troops tend to leave all their equipment, with the exception of their weapons and fly home. In the case of the Americans they drove every single vehicle out of the country and the incoming troops drove their own vehicles into the country. That goes part of the way to explaining why it took them three months to change over. Finally, a look at the names of the military camps in Baghdad summed up the gung ho attitude of the forces from the top downwards. We were based in Camp Victory and next to Camp Victory is Camp Slayer. Every military vehicle that drove about had its own regimental nickname etched on it, such as the Grim Reapers, the Slayers of Evil or Death Stalkers - hardly a blue print for winning over the hearts and minds of the local populace.

Money for the Americans, was no object and they were good at laying on entertainment. In November we had the cheerleaders from an American Football team which I unfortunately missed. Before Christmas I managed to catch some WWF wrestlers. I did find it difficult to get excited about someone pretending to hit his opponent over the head with a chair, but whooping and a hollering was fantastic. We saw the wrestlers wandering around the airport the following day and when we were offered autographs it was too tempting to say thank you to 'Giant Haystacks' and 'Big

Daddy'. I understood that their department was muscles but the wrestlers did seem to lack a sense of humour so we made a quick exit as a rather high pitched, steroid induced, growl followed in our wake.

Some good news in December was that Ziad's uncle was released from prison. Having been in jail for 95 days he left clutching a receipt for $10k, only $90k short of what was actually taken from him. However he was so relieved to be back with his family that he was not going to protest his innocence for fear of being thrown in jail again. It was no wonder the security situation had deteriorated. By this stage those that had sat on the fence when the Coalition first came into Iraq were no doubt playing a more active role against them. The bad guys were now targeting the airport with large rockets in an attempt to hit the terminal. If they managed this it would have been a political disaster and would have slowed the process of opening the airport yet further. The precursor for a rocket attack was a series of sirens that tended to go off around the camp. Unfortunately the warning sirens usually occurred at around the time of impact, or post impact. This wasn't much use to anyone and merely acted as an unnecessary disruption to a good nights sleep. A salvo in December was slightly closer to home. I was at a party at the FBI house with a couple of the more robust members of staff. We returned in the early hours to a group of very anxious employees who did not appreciate us being away when the action was occurring. The FBI party was a regular Saturday night fixture and there were other agencies that had them throughout the rest of the week. These happened in the houses/minor palaces that were seized and occupied by the agencies. Typically those with a villa would try to out do those with a small palace and the result was some excellent entertainment for the guests. At the FBI house I was shown Uday Hussein's yellow Porsche Carrera. It was acquired when they first entered the airport, no doubt rescued from the hangar of Uday's cars that were 'burned' to the ground. Apparently he used to drive around Baghdad in it and wind down the windows to shoot any unfortunate passers by. Interestingly we had ventured there under the pretext of being with a posse from the Iraq Survey Group. I asked the obvious question when I met them and yes, they were still searching for WMDs and the world was going to have to wait until August 2004 for the final report. They would admit though that there had been some mission creep and the focus was now on the biological and chemical proliferation of weapons post the conflict. A hungover Sunday was broken up by a barbecue at the control tower with the Australians. Entertainment was provided by some British Chinook pilots who, lacking a car, had flown the two miles from the other side of the airport and proceeded to drape a huge Union Jack flag out of the rear door as they headed home.

Due to the increasing missile attacks we had a brief interlude of no flights into Baghdad and a C5 (a huge military aircraft) was shot down. Luckily the missile only destroyed one of the four engines and so it landed safely with its load of 54 passengers. They were all unharmed with the exception of one who sprained his ankle getting out of the plane. In the post incident interviews the soldier, mindful that they are awarded a purple heart (medal) if they were wounded in action, took the opportunity to play up his distress and is now going to be awarded a purple heart! Following the incident on 22nd November we were forced to switch carriers and had some Turks flying in for us. The pilots used to fly

F16 fighter jets and found the idea of flying into a dangerous area quite exciting. It also meant that as the aircraft door opened and after the Turkish cigarette smoke cleared, two Turkish Tom Cruises would emerge. They would proceed to try and chat up the Iraqi female staff by offering them fresh croissants and soft drinks; a novel approach and not altogether successful.

There wasn't a day that went by without me thinking about how lucky the pilots were in our downed aircraft. A search on the internet, looking for any information about the DHL plane, revealed a chat net, involving soldiers who had been at the plane shortly after it came down. Amusingly they were playing up there role in the 'rescue' which was strange as I didn't remember seeing them at the scene. I should imagine there were several hundred 'rescuers' that now claim to have saved the lives of the pilots. Incidentally I have heard that all the crew are flying again and were airborne within a week, the theory following the same lines as falling off a horse - you need to get back on as soon as possible. Aircraft problems dogged us with the Antonovs but hope and humour was injected into the situation with Sergei's return to the fray. I first knew he was coming when I spotted the familiar sight of his green striped Antonov spluttering into sight as he spiraled down to the airport, belching smoke. The planes were under strict instructions to spiral in and out on take off so that they remained within the airport perimeter as now two had been shot down since ours on 22nd November and there have been numerous near misses. Sergei's mob came to a halt, the steps were thrown out of the door and Sergei came bounding towards me. Not quite 'Cadburys' Flake, misty, slow-motion footage but as near as you can get to on a runway in Baghdad. It was good to see him and following a series of bear hugs I was able to catch up with the news of his six weeks off with the family in Moldova. The hard drinking captain was missing and I asked after him. I was surprised and saddened to hear that he had just died of a heart attack. Admittedly this was a man who drank himself into a stupor every night and smoked every waking moment, but he was only 49. I was to miss his gold toothed grin and my attempts at trying to describe the weather in Mosul to him each morning. Also my surprise that a phony Russian accent seemed to help the translation process although I dare say the joke was on me.

18 LOCAL CUSTOM

Business culture varies from one country to another. It is important to familiarise yourself with local custom to avoid embarrassment, show respect, and solidify emerging relationships.

(The Encyclopedia of Current Business Orthodoxy)

'Ladies and Gentlemen... we got him.' Paul Bremer was of course referring to the capture of Saddam Hussein. I was actually in London at the time on Christmas leave and had received a call as I was standing at Fulham Broadway tube station. A colleague in Tikrit had rung to tell me that the Coalition Forces had captured Saddam about ten miles south of Tikrit. I let out a delighted yell of pleasure and got onto the next tube itching to tell the besuited commuters but realised they would probably think I was mad. Just my luck that I was in the UK. There was going to be shooting in the streets of Baghdad that night. If the reaction to the capture of his sons was anything to go by, there would be some spectacular fireworks, Iraqi style. I only hoped that they were a little more careful this time - and that spectators remained indoors.

How was this going to change things? There was undoubtedly a collective sigh of relief amongst Iraqis. The manner of his capture also went some way to explode the Saddam myth. I doubted that it would be the end to the bombings and resistance. I didn't think many commentators were/are under the illusion that he was masterminding a terrorist backlash against the coalition. The anti coalition forces may have been his supporters but as many of them came from Syria and Iran, across the open borders, it was likely that his removal would do little to halt the flow of blood. Even if the borders were sealed off and access was controlled there would still be problems. It may sound trite to draw comparisons with former Soviet Bloc countries like Yugoslavia, but there are definitely similarities when one looks at the religious and ethnic issues that angrily simmered under the control of a dictator. Iraq had a Sunni minority that enjoyed the patronage of Saddam and ran his country, filling many of the positions of authority. The Shia majority were abused, downtrodden and neglected. In the North the Kurdish issue and their cries for independence could be added to the concoction. These are clearly the main protagonists. Add to this the wave of Iraqis who fled the country and have since come back to claim a seat in the executive. Then understand that the average Iraqi views the latter group with huge distrust and distaste. They resent the fact that whilst they suffered in Iraq these wannabe leaders enjoyed life outside the country in safety and comfort, with three meals a day. Finally bear in mind everyone who wants revenge or feels that they have been dealt with unjustly and you have a situation that requires a severe adjustment of the American vision of democracy if peace is going to have a chance. In Eastern Europe there are countless examples of the removal of a dictator resulting in a blood bath as the potential replacements vied for the vacant slot. In Iraq there are those that want the coalition removed so that they can fill the empty position. Cynical though it may sound, I doubted that many of the politicians in Iraq were really doing it for the good of the people.

The corruption was not as bad as I would imagine it to be elsewhere in the world because people just expected to take a small share of your business. On one occasion a contractor offered me a $2500 bribe to accept his quote for some building work. I was irritated and he looked at me as if I was mad when I told him I would be accepting someone else's quote, not least because it was 20% lower than his. He responded by trying to kill off the competition who then became too frightened to come and do the work. So to persuade them to come to work they needed some more money and before I knew it we'd only saved 5% rather than 20%. That same day I discovered that the forklifts we had ordered were stuck in customs because the relevant people had not been paid off. The icing on the cake was that the American Air Force, who had been providing some forklifts sent me an email telling me we would be unable to use them from the start of next week. In theory this meant we would be unloading 200 tons of freight a day by hand! Some serious begging/pizza offering ensued and a stay of execution was given on the forklift removal.

It was whilst visiting the Air Force that the subject of missiles came up and I discovered that the US had been buying them off the black market at $500 a missile. They believed that the January increase in price to $750 each heralded a reduction in the quantity of missiles available on the market. Perhaps not, I suggested, as there were apparently 3000 in Iraq prior to 1991 and no one knew how many had entered the country since then. The fact that they had bought a thousand or so hardly gave me, or the pilots, a warm fuzzy feeling. I could see I had upset them when I had the cheek to suggest that the ex-General who was their tout may be getting greedy or may be running out of his personal supply. As well as the $500 per missile he got a 'cash reward' per missile and a car and a telephone. I didn't ask if he got health insurance and a pension as they would have thought I was serious. I was barely able to stop myself laughing out aloud when they told me that he also gave them intelligence for which they paid him. He had delivered a gem, for example, on New Years Eve when he forewarned a number of attacks on the airport with the flakey tip off to the military that they 'would have problems sleeping tonight'. I likened it to reading my daily horoscope, with predictions vague enough to allow for anything from alien invasion to Grandma burning the toast.

We had now left the culinary delights of Edmundo's 'missed grill' in the Flowers Land Hotel and were living in a portacabin village at the airport. I didn't really relish the prospect of living in a portacabin but as the security situation had deteriorated so much we were left with no option. The Flowers Land Hotel was opposite a hotel full of journalists and other westerners. Both hotels had gone some way to increase the security, installing huge concrete blast walls in addition to the usual armed guards. But my greatest fear of a car bomb still lingered and in all honesty I did not think the Iraqi set up was sufficient enough to prevent a determined attack. Furthermore, the nightly shooting in the street outside and the mortaring of the Coalition Provisional Authority, which was only across the river did little to lighten the mood. In fact the decision was vindicated when the car bomb went off at Nabil's restaurant on New Years Eve, which was just around the corner from the hotel and somewhere we passed regularly.

The cabins were OK; a shipment of Ikea's choicest furniture offset the grey metal walls and tartan rugs. The water worked intermittently and we fed ourselves on the leftovers from Christmas: cheese, mince pies, sausages, biscuits, Christmas puddings, custard and more cheese. In fact, it was rather like being a student just without the long lie-ins. We also managed to acquire a couple of dogs from the zoo. The zoo was full of strays that the military handed in when they departed so Jack and Oi arrived. A little dog house was built to cope with their nasty habit of ending up in our rooms halfway through the night and then crapping on the floor. (On one occasion Jack managed to lay a turd on Phil's bed whilst he was asleep). They were good guards but took to their new role with rather too much zeal. They seemed to spend an awful lot of time barking at anything from gunfire to helicopters so sleep was fitful. We also discovered that we were remarkably unprepared on the food front for the dogs. As a result they ate a lot of Christmas puddings, mince pies and ambrosia custard. Before the RSPCA got called in, we managed to wean them off the Christmas pudding but they went through a stage of insisting on having custard on their dog biscuit. There was a very interesting relationship between Iraqis and dogs. They simply thought they were dirty animals and should barely be tolerated so found our fascination with the animals rather disconcerting. There was no love lost from the side of the dogs either - they soon became rather racist when choosing who deserved a growl. This caused a few problems for our local security guard who clearly wanted to give the dogs a good thrashing but knew that it is not the done thing, so ended up laughing through clenched teeth as the dogs chased him around the compound.

With the dog food came pizza, just in time for New Year's Eve. Generally flying pizza from Bahrain to Iraq is not the most cost effective way of acquiring a take away, but it was New Year's Eve. We also managed to acquire some Iraqi champagne and various other strange liqueurs. Dinner was prepared but promptly delayed when it was realised that the newly constructed tables were a little tall. By the time the legs had been shortened - too much - dinner was cold.

The New Year celebrations showed us another side of the US army. I had always heard about areas on aircraft carriers that were ghettos and were accessed by invitation only. We found our way to the army equivalent. Fortunately we got a verbal 'yo' which was all we needed, though I think the vodka and champagne we had tucked under our arms may have eased our entrance. The room we went into was extraordinary. It was like the tardis. The entrance was through the front of a shipping container and then we went out of the side of it into a wooden construction that was built as an extension containing a bar and dance floor. The waft of dope hit me as we entered and through the gloom I could see various people dancing. We joined in the spirit of things and proceeded to drink our contribution to the evening. Come New Year we were an incongruous bunch singing Auld Lang Syne whilst others hollered and whooped the New Year in. There then followed an enormous amount of back slapping and amusingly complicated handshakes.

In our humourous state we decided that between the four of us a little dance competition was in order as we were sure this was what they would be doing in the Bronx. Whilst three stood round in a circle the fourth had to strut his stuff resulting in a variety of poorly executed break dancing moves, some even poorer moon walking and numerous shuffling numbers accompanied with waving arms and cheesy grins. Meanwhile the remaining three were crying with laughter and having difficulty standing. Sure enough the humour was lost on some and a full blown dance-off developed. We were way out of our depth so did not take up the gauntlet but instead went back to the car to sing. It started with carols, took in some of Vinod's (our new IT guru) Indian songs, and inevitably ended in any song we knew the words to. For some reason the 12 days of Christmas featured strongly. Memory was not good though and so the ninth day became nine Hum Vs. At about 2.30am an irritated soldier tried to bribe us with some horse tranquilisers to get us to shut up. We declined his kind offer, sang a couple more songs and wandered off to our cabins.

On returning we were greeted by the sight of a security guard dressed in a Christmas hat who had clearly made up for a late start on the drinking front. He slithered through the mud with the puppies yapping at his heels. We tended to keep the dogs down at the accommodation because they were a little unruly and run all over the runway. We also wanted to avoid a repeat of an accident in Mosul where one of the Tristar pilots ran over the puppy. The boys in Mosul had wondered where it had got to and it wasn't until the pilot came in to the office and greeted them with 'your fackin' dog is wrapped around my wheels' that they realized that 'Poochy' had gone for good.

2004 started as it meant to continue. The Antonov crew flew into Baghdad and quickly took off again for Mosul. I waited for their call to confirm arrival and began to fret once they had overshot the schedule by two hours. They eventually called and explained casually that they had been 'delayed'. Further questioning revealed they had actually got lost! An unscheduled Tristar then landed in Baghdad and I went to talk to the crew who turned out not to be the puppy murderers but a charming father and son combo. The father was very pleased with himself and went on to tell me that his son was 30 and the youngest of two... until he had another child last year. Not sure whether to be surprised or impressed I asked the son if he got on with his one year old sibling much and he joked about finding it difficult as a middle child.

Despite Saddam's capture there had been no sudden change in the security situation. I bumped into General Sir Michael Rose who was busy explaining to an American soldier why a guardsman would always have a tie on. He had spent an interesting couple of days on a fact finding mission in Basra and Baghdad and was under the impression that despite the political spin the military were putting on the situation, things were not quite what they seemed. I don't know whether it had come through in the UK press but the conspiracy theories had begun over the capture of Saddam. At first there was a Bahraini paper that decided the trees in the background of the photo would not have had dates on at that time of year and therefore the photo had been taken earlier. A more credible version was that Saddam was actually held captive by his own body guards. It is believed that they held him in the hole and used an ex General to negotiate the ransom. Saddam emerged from his hole, looking like he did because the US decided they were going to try to track him down through the go-between, which took several weeks. Whether they managed this or simply paid the ransom is conjecture but it does explain the state he was in when he was captured. Evidently he believed he was being rescued so it really was a case of out of the frying pan and into the fire.

The security situation had actually been deteriorating on the roads and I had had a near escape in January. On a return trip from visiting the office in Balad I was overtaking a car that swerved in front of me causing me to hit it and causing our second vehicle to hit the back of me. I briefed the guys on the radio to stand by and keep an eye out for trouble. I got out of our armoured vehicle and walked over to see the owners of the car. There was no damage to their vehicle but needless to say they knew a money making opportunity when they saw one. There followed a lot of crying, wailing and shouting to Allah. I have found the best approach in this situation was to wait until they calmed down or realised that they were not going to get a reaction from me. This was the point at which you could see them weighing up their options and the situation could go either way. The wailing had stopped. It was time for decisions from both parties. I could almost read their minds as their eyes flicked from one vehicle to the next and back to me. They were trying to work out if a) we were armed - which we were not and b) if so, were we likely to use weapons in the event of some trouble. By now a crowd began to form around me and I was aware that things were rapidly going pear-shaped particularly when one of them approached me brandishing a metal bar. I needed to difuse the situation quickly and so I took the driver away from the crowd and produced a series of small notes from my pocket. He recognized the notes but was unsure of their value. Whilst he was working his way through the best part of $30 in small change I hopped into the vehicle and we drove off. The following day a contractor was shot and killed on the same stretch of road. This stretch of road became infamous and proved to be a real pain in the arse on the business front as truck drivers started to refuse to drive to Balad because of the risks.

The situation was made worse when one of our convoys witnessed a truck in front of them being shot at and the driver getting hit. Admittedly he was hit in the backside but it did little to calm their nerves. Money helped but was not a long term solution and once you pay a man an extra $10 it was very difficult to take it away from him at a later date. Endless cups of tea, conversation, smutty jokes and cigarettes seemed to be a little more productive. More often than not it was acknowledgement of the task that they were doing coupled with an ego boosting chat that clinched the deal. Having persuaded them to do the journey I did feel slightly guilty when I subsequently heard that there had been several explosions on the road and that military convoys had been turning back. Natural hazards combined to increase the road problems. Every now and then it rained, the dust turned to mud and the combination of bald tyres, oil, mud and water made the roads lethal. On a return trip from Balad one day, we saw nine dead dogs, three serious accidents and two dead people all in the space of about 60 miles.

Every time there was an incident in Baghdad it touched someone we knew. Whether it was the mechanic, whose car was gutted by the New Years Eve restaurant bomb, or the bombing of the Iraqis queuing to work in the CPA. Whenever these things happened it was a step backwards. Our CPA employee was a couple of minutes late for work that day. Fortunately she was not standing chatting to her two friends who had arrived on time and were brutally murdered. Understandably she had reservations about going back to work the following day and so we drove her in with us.

That she was still keen to work with us was testament to the commitment and loyalty the Iraqis had shown us since they became employees. Of course they were fortunate to have a job but I was not the one who couldn't tell my neighbours where I worked. I was not the one who had to change out of my work clothes before I left in the evening and I was not the one who was abused and threatened by passers by when I stood to go into the camps. Combine that with the ever present threat of a suicide bomber and I found myself admiring their perseverance, good nature and ability to laugh and joke throughout the day. This was epitomised by a lovely habit they had of congregating at the end of the day, the couriers, the warehouse staff and the Customer Services girls. They then spent the next 30 minutes having a laugh and a chat about the day's proceedings before getting into their minibuses and driving home.

I became ever more aware of the siege mentality that the coalition forces had adopted. More and more concrete blocks were erected on a daily basis. Having found my way through the maze of concrete into the CPA I noticed that this feeling had permeated throughout the building as the once open spaces were now enclosed as offices with combination locks on every door. Gone were the days of breezing along the corridors in flip flops and shorts and sticking my head around a ministry door to have a chat. Everyone was now hidden out of sight until the occasional burst of activity saw them stride purposefully from one combination door lock to the next. It was easy to tell the newcomers as they fumbled with the locks, unsure of the codes, blushed and scampered back to their origin to email a colleague for the right code. Outside the palace the lawns were now filled with tents surrounded by hastily erected sandbag walls promising protection from the regular mortar fire. Having scoffed at their paranoia I checked my email and found a summary of the security incidents for 30th December. It was sobering reading particularly when compared to the summaries that were being put out six months ago.

Summary of Security incidents (30 Dec)

- In the absence of military targets, terrorists have demonstrated that they will strike civilian targets. Terrorist attacks will continue focusing on targets intended to undermine coalition cohesion, intimidate the Iraqi Governing Council (IGC) and demoralize coalition partners and non-governmental organisations (NGOs). Throughout Iraq attacks will continue to focus on civilian and military targets in an effort to undermine coalition cohesion. The targeting includes IGC members, government facilities and Iraqi Police and police stations.
- Improvised explosive devices (IEDs) continue to be the biggest threat to coalition forces followed by small arms fire and mortar attacks although the use of rockets is increasing in popularity. Anti coalition elements will continue to use missiles, car bombs and improvised rockets, while seeking new ways to escalate their campaign against the coalition. The effects of the attacks will be most acutely felt in terms of public perception of coalition success in Iraq, not in terms of actual impact on the coalition operations. (This represented a huge change in tack.)
- Saddam's arrest has increased Iraqi expectations that life will be better. This could result in disappointments

in the short to mid term if issues such as the fuel crisis, electricity difficulties, security situation, unemployment rate and economic problems do not show signs of improvement.

NORTH

- A unit was attacked with mortar and small arms fire north of Al Qayyarah at 2100hrs
- A base in Mosul was targeted with Mortar fire at 2030hrs
- Mosul airfield was targeted with mortar fire at 2000hrs
- A unit 12km south of Hammam Al Alil near Al Qayyarah was targeted with mortar fire at 1900hrs
- A unit in Tall Afar was attacked with mortar fire at 1800hrs
- An off duty soldier was shot and killed near a brick manufacturing company in the industrial quarter of Irbil by suspects in a red VW Brasilli at 1730hrs
- A bomb exploded near Balad airbase at 1700hrs. The device was a 130mm mortar round and remotely detonated
- A patrol was attacked with small arms fire from a rooftop in Tikrit and were then mortared at 1700hrs
- Several suspects were detained for possession of hand grenades north east of Mandali near the Iranian border at 1500hrs
- A convoy was attacked by suspects in a blue sedan while travelling south of Balad on highway one at 1400hrs
- A patrol shot at a suspect in Mosul believed to be shooting at them on 1230hrs. Suspect was actually shooting at other family members

- A bomb was found near Jalula near the Iranian border
- A convoy was ambushed when several bombs exploded from both sides of the road, followed by small arms fire west of Balad at 1000hrs
- A suspect with a knife was shot when he attempted to stab a soldier at the Ashur Bank in Mosul at 0930hrs
- A unit observed mortar fire originating from east of Balad at 0930hrs

BAGHDAD

- A unit was attacked with small arms fire whilst on foot near the Palestine Hotel at 2200hrs
- A bomb was discovered on the highway in the east of Baghdad. The device was a 130mm mortar round with bricks on top
- A patrol was ambushed when a bomb exploded west of Baghdad at 2100hrs. The assailant fled in a Bongo truck
- A unit was attacked with small arms fire to the east of the Tigris at 1900hrs. The assailants fled in a bus (last two get away vehicles not too impressive)
- An armored patrol was ambushed when a bomb exploded in the NE of Baghdad at 1530hrs
- A convoy was ambushed when a bomb exploded along the highway in the north west of the city at 1430hrs
- A unit shot at an armed suspect in the west of the city at 1400hrs
- A convoy was attacked when a bomb exploded in west Baghdad at 0900hrs

- A Kellog Brown and Root (civilian contractors) was ambushed when a bomb exploded in north west of the capital, killing the driver at 0900hrs

WEST

- A unit near the Syrian border in Husaybah was attacked with RPG, small arms and mortar fire at 1900hrs
- A bomb was discovered south of Ar Ramadi at 1630hrs
- A convoy was ambushed when a bomb exploded near Abu Ghuryab at 1430hrs
- A bomb was discovered 20 metres off the highway north of Ar Ramadi at 1400hrs
- A convoy was attacked when a bomb was exploded followed by small arms fire east of Al Fallujah at 1100hrs

SOUTH

- A bomb was discovered on the Latifiyah to Dourah crude pipeline
- Looters moved into a base and then to the university in Karbala at 1300hrs

19 MANAGING MORALE

A good manager's relationship with his or her staff extends beyond the purely professional but stops short of the purely personal. It is caring and concerned without being interfering or intimate. On occasions this requires extreme delicacy and sensitivity; providing support without allowing for the development of any dependency.

(The Encyclopedia of Current Business Orthodoxy)

In the run up to my departure the frenzied farewells seemed to increase as the final day drew near. I had not really thought about what DHL represented to our Iraqi employees. DHL had provided a sense of stability to the 47 Iraqi employees and the recently recruited security contingent we had brought over from Nepal. To these two groups my leaving rocked the boat a little and made them less confident about what lay ahead. My initial reaction to these sentiments was to think that they were being over dramatic but the more I dwelt on their fears the more I understood their reasoning. I had been in Iraq since the beginning and had recruited them into DHL. These Iraqis had never worked in their lives and we were their first contact with the west, its culture and its work ethic. In fact most of them had never even been to the airport before as it had remained closed to all but the privileged few. The deteriorating security situation merely accentuated their fears and inevitably they wanted to cling to what was familiar. I tried to mollify them with promises of my return and constant correspondence but it did little to lift their gloom.

The level of attacks had increased significantly but so had the US success rate at preventing these attacks. They had been deploying their Unmanned Aerial Vehicles to good effect. On one occasion they had watched a team of terrorists move into a firing position, watched them attempt to fire their rockets and had then followed them back to their house where they were later arrested. But in spite of these successes and having always been aware of the pops and bangs that were the background noise, I suddenly found myself being more conscious of them as my contract drew to a close. I was often asked how we coped with the constant gunfire and explosions. Was I in constant fear? A useful analogy is to look at it as if you are driving a car. Remember back to when you were first learning to drive and ventured onto the motorway for the first time. I remember listening to every nuance of the engine, feeling every bump in the road and watching other drivers as if they were going to deliberately crash into me. At the slightest hint of a bump, an engine grumble, or a swerving car my hands would tighten on the wheel and I would overcompensate on the brakes or change lane. As time went on, however, I relaxed more, no less aware of the potential hazard of crashes but more realistic about the chances of them involving me. What's more, I could limit the chance of these problems by driving sensibly, trying to predict the behaviour of other drivers and driving according to the weather conditions. Life in Iraq was very similar. I no longer flinched or was tempted to run for cover when I heard the bangs. They became a part of everyday life. What I tried to do was to predict likely hotspots and periods and then minimise the risk for everyone. On a personal level I then mixed in a healthy dose of fatalism and got on with work, remaining as flexible as possible. It was this flexibility mixed in with a stubborn determination that really enabled us to trounce our competitors.

The Iraq operation was well supported by John Chisholm and a couple of key individuals in Bahrain, our head office. They could see the strategic importance of Iraq and of course the money that could be made. The strength of this collective will was particularly evident following the shooting down of the plane. Those who were outside the Middle East wanted DHL out of Iraq at once. A process of gentle persuasion with a healthy measure of steely resolve enabled us to find more aircraft and continue with what we were doing. Underlying this was a review of the security side of the operation and a further analysis of the risks. Shortly after the plane had come down, I had covered the hole in the wing and the DHL had been painted off the side I remember thinking that we had successfully limited the publicity. Fortunately the event coincided with England winning the world cup, which helped to mask our drama. Needless to say photos of the aircraft appeared in Middle Eastern papers and on the internet but in this case it merely acted as positive publicity. A week after the event we had resumed our service and talk about harbouring customer loyalty, we had cornered the market on that front. We had certainly earned their respect and commitment to use our service. It was this unswerving resolve to maintain the service that really won the hearts of the customers. We were also helped by the fact that the expectations were not excessively high. Those that were working in Iraq certainly understood that the service may face glitches and the plane being shot down was certainly one of these glitches. Our organisational recipe had proved a success and the DHL maxim of not farming the work out to agencies had really proved its validity. Various competitors had taken this route and it was making business very difficult for them.

The official farewells began with a drink with the Nepalese and a moving speech from their supervisor, Tulsi. The following day the build up to the employee party was heralded by a succession of visits to my office. A series of trinkets started to be given to me. I was adorned with bracelets, rings and necklaces and these were clearly required to be worn, certainly until my departure. I couldn't help feeling that I looked at best like Mr. T from the A Team, or a 70's porn star at worst. But this was only the start. They then produced gold jewelry for my fiancé Anna, someone they had not even met. Their generosity left me lost for words. It was humbling to think that these were people that we paid $300 a month and they could still find the money to spend on gold bracelets and rings. It epitomised the warm and generous nature of the Iraqi people. These were a people who were desperate for security, they craved the prosperity that had been snatched away from them at the end of the Iraq Iran war and before the first Gulf War and they dearly wanted a return to normal life. The feeling was that they would achieve this but it was going to be a longer and more tortuous road than they had envisaged. They had begun to understand that the removal of Saddam was actually only the start of the process and was not the panacea that pre war coalition propaganda may have led them to believe.

I left Iraq as I had arrived, in the Antonov. Sergei and his crew had recently returned and with their new captain Igor

Smirnoff at the controls I boarded the plane. It all seemed to be going remarkably smoothly and then just as I started boarding the plane a mini drama unfolded. We had contracted the escorting of our trucks to an Iraqi security company and they would come down to the airport each day to pick up the trucks. This was further backed up by a satellite tracking device that we fitted to the escort vehicles so that we could trace their movement. The cars had parked one behind the other and one of the systems had been fitted. They were due to depart and their boss was standing between the front and rear of the two cars. The rear driver turned the car on and rather than putting it into reverse, slipped it into first and sped forward to trap his boss between the bumper of both cars, breaking his knee cap. Much to his annoyance we cut his jeans off and splinted his leg before sticking him into the ambulance and taking him to hospital. The drama over, the staff gave me a fabulous send off, lining the apron as we taxied onto the runway. I say 'we' because I was at the controls in the co-pilot's seat. I had joked that Igor should let me be his co-pilot and sure enough there I was taxiing the plane for take off whilst the real co-pilot buzzed around me tapping dials and flicking switches. Igor gave me my instructions over the headphones, as we lined up at the start of the runway, under starters orders. The only thing he wanted me to do was to pull back on the joystick when he told me to. The props were cranked up and we started to shudder down the runway, picking up speed rapidly. I was given the nod, Igor adjusted the trim, and I eased back on the joystick and we lifted into the air. I waved goodbye to Baghdad and we headed off into the distance.

As we flew I was given a basic lesson on the highway code, planes flying west to east fly at an even altitude and east to west at an odd. As the navigator it was really Sergei's job to look out for other aircraft and he was ideally positioned as he sat in the glass nose of the plane with a set of binoculars and a map. Also I quickly realised that looking at the horizon was not the sensible way to fly as I quickly got disorientated and sent us into a slight dive. The dials were the key to a smoother journey. Having mastered this the captain then switched on his mini DVD player, propped it on the instrument panel and settled down to Tom Hanks in Castaway which I found slightly disconcerting. As we left Iraqi airspace I handed the controls back to their rightful owner who looked mightily relieved. I went to relax in the passenger area which had been updated with a new marble effect linoleum that strangely covered everything but the floor. There was a bench and a table and the flight attendant (engineer in Y fronts) served me a cup of coffee and my in flight meal, a frankfurter that had been boiled in the kettle. Pudding was a shot of vodka and a selection of pick and mix sweets which had been stolen from my office! Content, I settled back and before long we had arrived in Bahrain without any problems. The crew changed into their uniforms and parked next to the other Antonov that had recently returned from a flight to Kabul. The crew was repainting the plane and I asked Sergei why they didn't just wash it. The response was that it takes the whole crew, of seven, two days to wash it but it only takes five of them one day to repaint it. It got repainted twice a year and was about 27 years old. I commented that with a few extra kilos per coat the plane must have got a little heavier. The response a shrug and 'at least you can tell how old it is when you cut it in half.'

20 EPILOGUE - APRIL 2004

I soon had the opportunity to return to Baghdad. It was a chance that I jumped at. Iraq was suffering from a hammering in the press as the security situation had deteriorated. The press referred to it as a 'general uprising' occurring throughout the country. The flight into Baghdad Airport involved the usual roller coaster approach as we spiralled sharply down to the runway. Upon arrival, I was greeted by the emotional DHL staff who I think were pleasantly surprised to see me back. Following a brief conversation with them it was clear that the press had some basis for their claims and things had indeed got worse. There was an almost tangible fear amongst the Iraqis who had been awoken that morning by the call for prayer. This was not unusual but there was a worrying development. Booming over the speakers was a call for the Shia and Sunni to march together against the coalition. As I contemplated the enormity of this, my ears tuned into the background noise of gunfire that I had grown unaccustomed to in my short absence. I could clearly hear the heavy artillery pounding Fallujah. A hot spot, it had now been encircled by the US Marines following the brutal murder of four security contractors the previous week. These security guards were beginning a new contract as the previous security contractors believed the route had become too dangerous. The advice was to avoid the road, but as usual in Iraq, some money was thrown at the problem, all sense was blinded and they took on the contract. They decided to recce the route to Fallujah but they never stood a chance, the ambush had been set. Some children crossed the road in front of the lead vehicle to slow the convoy and three rocket propelled grenades (RPGs) were fired into the rear vehicle. The occupants were killed immediately. The crowd rejoiced and took the bodies out of the vehicles to parade them around the town. These were the images that were seen in the world's press. It was these images that acted as the catalyst to the marine crackdown on the town. Fallujah had always had a reputation as being a dangerous area for coalition forces and contractors but I was surprised that it had deteriorated so rapidly. One of the local Sheiks told me that despite coming from the town he had been warned to stay away by the fighters within. He went on to say that although there were some Iraqis in Fallujah the majority were foreign fighters from Syria and Iran.

The problem was not limited to Fallujah. There was a power struggle going on throughout the rest of the country and pockets of violence affecting both the military and civilians were contributing to the general and profound feeling of unease. There were also rumours of rioting in Baghdad. The Iraqi employees were becoming agitated and nervous so I felt the best way to quash the rumours was to go and have a look for myself. I was still reluctant to believe that everything had deteriorated so quickly. We donned body armour and set off in convoy in our armoured vehicles and headed for the CPA. Sadly the use of body armour and armoured vehicles had become the norm; it was simply too unsafe to operate in any other way. Civilian contractors were a prime target and this was one of the ways we could reduce our exposure.

The airport road into town is only a 20 minute drive but we were briefed that there had been a sharp increase in the number of attacks on the road. The Coalition were struggling to maintain any form of security on this stretch of road as it had become a prime target for the terrorists. They had realised that those on the road were likely to be doing work for the coalition and were therefore a 'legitimate' target. I confess I had a slight feeling of dread as I clambered into my car and the various scenarios of what may lie ahead spun through my mind. We drove out through the protective concrete barriers that marked the end of the safe zone around the airport. I put my foot flat to the floor and we sped along the motorway. The roads were worryingly deserted, never a good sign as it made me feel even more of a target. Rounding a corner I noticed a large crowd of demonstrators seated on the hard shoulder, under the watchful eyes of three soldiers. Further up the road we passed a burning 4x4 vehicle, much like our own. It had just been hit by RPGs. This certainly focused the mind and we continued along the road to the first set of check points that marked the entrance to the 'green zone'. Having shown our ID, I had a brief chat with the soldiers and then passed through the chicanes and second set of check points. My pulse slowed as we had arrived in the comparatively safe confines of the CPA.

Once inside the CPA it was business as usual and I went to meet the new Minister for Transport to find out the latest and I popped my head through the door of a couple of other Ministries to say hello to some old friends. I was keen to find out what they felt would be the outcome of the impending elections particularly in light of the current scenario. Earlier in the day, the view our Iraqi employees had taken was that an Iraqi government would make no difference. This was echoed in the CPA. It was explained that although the Iraqis had the final vote on any law, the CPA still controlled the purse strings and if they disagreed with the vote the money would be withheld. There was a feeling that the Iraqis in positions of power were already trying to distance themselves from the Coalition and thus strengthen their own position. It was going to be interesting to see how the relationship between Iraqi minister and CPA minister worked with these restrictions. I really believed that it was the first important step in the right direction and if managed carefully could lead to a return to a degree of autonomy for Iraq. Whether this would happen was clearly up to the Americans. Sir Jeremy Greenstock had recently announced his return to the UK, despite Blair's requests for him to stay put. He declined Blair's invitation as he had clearly been left out of the decision-making process of the CPA and felt that this was a situation that was not going to change. I would imagine that he felt he may as well return to the UK rather than waste his time in Baghdad. If that was how uninvolved a major ally was, I wondered how an Iraqi executive would fare. It will be interesting to see how the planned elections go in January 2005. I think there will be considerable unrest as the parties jostle for power and the terrorists try and prevent them taking place at all. The CPA had also realised the potential problem and were already referring to the date as 'tentative' thus allowing leeway for a change in the timescale.

The CPA was like a ghost town; gone was the hustle and bustle that we were used to. Gone was the spirit of optimism and buzz of excitement that echoed around the halls of the palace 12 months earlier. It was replaced with empty corridors and rooms crammed with people tapping away on their laptops. One thing was evident, Dell were doing a roaring trade. But the feeling of everyone being intrepid explorers was replaced by a realisation that there was a mountain to climb. I stopped for a quick pee in Saddam's loo and whilst standing at the urinal was aware of a muddle of people behind me. I was joined on my right by none other than Ambassador Bremer, to whom I gave a polite nod. I could hear his security shifting around behind me and having overcome my stage fright finished my business before walking out into the corridor. I was so busy chuckling to myself that I almost knocked over General Sanchez who was walking in the opposite direction. It reminded me what an extraordinary environment I had been working in, not because I pissed with the premier but because a month ago I wouldn't have given those two events a second thought. Our meetings were cut short by a phone call from Jo, the DHL security advisor, who rang us to tell us that the road to the airport was becoming blocked due to a demonstration of angry protestors. We needed to get back to the airport immediately. These protestors were the ones that we had seen sitting calmly by the road. We were told that shortly after we drove past the situation had got out of hand and they had knifed and killed one of the soldiers. My heart sank; this was the last thing I needed. I had a lot to achieve in the short time I was out there and was going to have to postpone several meetings as a result of our recall. So hearts in our mouths we returned to the airport. It was still relatively cool but I was sweating. As we drove over the brow of the hill to where the protestors had been on our journey in I said a little prayer. It must have been answered. The roads were empty, not a demonstrator in sight. We had not been told that following the death of the soldier the military had cleared the remainder of the demonstrators away.

Back at the Airport, the fourth Royal Jordanian plane of the day was taking off. They had recently increased their flights from one a day due to the overwhelming rush of civilian contractors attempting to flee the country. Many of the contractors had taken some timely leave and the thriving ex-pat community dwindled dramatically. In many respects it felt as if we were coming out to Iraq for the first time except this time it had all got a lot more serious. There was no going out in the evening; it was lock down. I felt it was time to visit my Australian friends in the control tower and find out when they were going to be handing the skies back to the Iraqis. Needless to say I was to discover that this process had been delayed. It was no fault of the Australians but simply down to the fact that they were unable to assess Iraqi air traffic controllers. The latter had refused to walk up the two hundred stairs to the top of the tower, the only option as the lift had not yet been repaired.

I returned to the office and heard more bad news. The Iraqis were not going to come to work for a couple of days as they feared for their lives when outside their houses. For the first time in a year I thought I could see the spark of life in their eyes growing dull. They were, however, buoyed by the fact that we had been into Baghdad but seemed unconvinced with my rather hollow sounding argument that it seemed to be getting better. Who could blame them? There I was peeling off body armour having just driven back in an armoured vehicle. It was a year ago to the day that we had first driven into Baghdad in a 'soft skinned' Land Rover wearing no more than the shirts on our backs and with a feeling of excitement and hope. Somehow I don't think this had been the planned outcome of the 'let's rescue Iraq' package hatched by the Coalition eighteen months previously.

About Eye Books

Eye books is a young, dynamic publishing company that likes to break the rules. Our independence allows us to publish books which challenge the way people see things. It also means that we can offer new authors a platform from which they can shine their light and encourage others to do the same.

To date we have published 30 books that cover a number of genres including Travel, Biography, Adventure and History. Many of our books are experience driven. All of them are inspirational and life-affirming.

Frigid Women, for example, tells the story of the world-record making first all female expedition to the North Pole. A fifty year-old mother of three who had recently recovered from a mastectomy, and her daughter are the authors neither had ever written a book before. Sue Riches is now both author and highly sought after motivational speaker.

We also publish thematic anthologies, such as The Tales from Heaven and Hell series, for those who prefer the short story format. Here everyone has the chance to get their stories published and win prizes such as flights to any destination in the world.

And here's what makes us really different: As well as publishing books, Eye Books has set up a club for like-minded people and is in the process of developing a number of initiatives and services for its community of members. After all, the more you put into life, the more you get out of it.

Please visit www.eye-books.com for further information.

Eye Club Membership

Each month, we receive hundreds of enquiries' from people who have read our books, discovered our website or entered our competitions. All of these people have certain things in common; a desire to achieve, to extend the boundaries of everyday life and to learn from others' experiences.

Eye Books has, therefore, set up a club to unite these like-minded people. It is a community where members can exchange ideas, contact authors, discuss travel, both future and past as well as receive information and offers from ourselves.

Membership is free.

Benefits of the Eye Club

As a member of the Eye Club:

• You are offered the invaluable opportunity to contact our authors directly.
• You will be able to receive a regular newsletter, information on new book releases and company developments as well as discounts on new and past titles.
• You can attend special member events such as book launches, author talks and signings.
• Receive discounts on a variety of travel related products and services from Eye Books partners.
• In addition, you can enjoy entry into Eye Books competitions including the ever popular Heaven and Hell series and our monthly book competition.

To register your membership, simply visit our website and register on our club pages: www.eye-books.com.

New Titles

Riding the Outlaw Trail - Simon Casson
A true story of an epic horseback journey by two Englishmen from
Mexico to Canada, across 2,000 miles of some of America's most
difficult terrain. Their objective? To retrace the footsteps of those
legendary real life bandits Butch Cassidy and the Sundance Kid, by
riding the outlaw trails they rode more than a century ago.
ISBN: 1 903070 228. Price £9.99.

Desert Governess - Phyllis Ellis
Phyllis, a former Benny Hill actress, takes on a new challenge when
she becomes a governess to the Saudi Arabian Royal family. In this
frank personal memoir, she gives us an insider's view into the Royal
family and a woman's role in this mysterious kingdom.
ISBN: 1 903070 015. Price £9.99.

Last of the Nomads - W. J. Peasley
Warri and Yatungka were the last of the desert nomads to live
permanently in the traditional way. Their deaths marked the end
of a tribal lifestyle that stretched back more than 30,000 years. The
Last of the Nomads tells of an extraordinary journey in search of
Warri and Yatungka, their rescue and how they survived alone for
thirty years in the unrelenting Western Desert region of Australia.
ISBN: 1 903070 325. Price £9.99.

All Will Be Well - Michael Meegan
So many self help books look internally to provide inspiration,
however this book looks at how love and compassion when given
out to others, can act as a better antidote to the human condition
than trying to inwardly solve feelings of discontentment.
ISBN: 1 903070 279. Price £9.99.

First Contact - Mark Anstice
This is a true story of a modern day exploration by two young adventurers and the discovery of cannibal tribes in the 21st century. An expedition far more extraordinary than they had ever imagined, one that would stretch them, their friendship and their equipment to the limits.
ISBN: 1 903070 260. Price £9.99.

Further Travellers' Tales From Heaven and Hell - Various
This is the third book in the series, after the first two best selling Travellers' Tales from Heaven and Hell. It is an eclectic collection of over a hundred anecdotal travel stories which will enchant you, shock you and leave you in fits of laughter!
ISBN: 1 903070 112. Price £9.99.

Special Offa - Bob Bibby
Following his last best selling book Dancing with Sabrina, Bob walks the length of Offa's Dyke. He takes us through the towns and villages that have sprung up close by and reveals their ancient secrets and folklore. He samples the modern day with his refreshingly simple needs and throws light on where to go and what to see.
ISBN: 1 903070 287. Price £9.99.

The Good Life - Dorian Amos
Needing a change and some adventure, Dorian and his wife searched their world atlas and decided to sell up and move to Canada. Having bought Pricey the car, Boris Lock their faithful dog, a canoe and their fishing equipment they set off into the Yukon Wilderness to find a place they could call home.
ISBN: 1 903070 309. Price £9.99.

Green Oranges on Lion Mountain - Emily Joy
Armed with a beginner's guide to surgery, GP Emily Joy took up
her VSO posting at a remote hospital in Sierra Leone. As she set off
into the unknown, action, adventure and romance were high on
her agenda; rebel forces and the threat of civil war were not.
ISBN: 1 903070 295. Price £9.99.

The Con Artist Handbook - Joel Levy
Get wise with The Con Artist's Handbook as it blows the lid on the
secrets of the successful con artist and his con games. Get inside
the hustler's head and find out what makes him tick; Learn how the
world's most infamous scams are set up and performed; Peruse the
career profiles of the most notorious scammers and hustlers of all time;
Learn to avoid the modern-day cons of the e-mail and Internet age.
ISBN: 1 903070 341. Price £9.99.

The Forensics Handbook - Pete Moore
The Forensic Handbook is the most up-to-date log of forensic
techniques available. Discover how the crime scene is examined
using examples of some of the most baffling crimes; Learn
techniques of lifting and identifying prints; Calculate how to
examine blood splatter patterns; Know what to look for when
examining explosive deposits, especially when terrorist activity is
suspected. Learn how the Internet is used to trace stalkers.
ISBN: 1 903070 35X. Price £9.99.

My Journey With A Remarkable Tree - Ken Finn
Ken set out exploring Cambodia to indulge his passion and
fascination with trees. What he found was certainly moving but in a
much bleaker way than he had ever imagined. His journey became
a mission as he followed his once remarkable tree from spirit forest
to the furniture corner of a garden centre.
ISBN: 1 903070 384. Price £9.99

Seeking Sanctuary - Hilda Reilly

Seeking Sanctuary tells the stories of a group of Muslim converts from the west who found liberation in Sudan. They describe their spiritual and physical journeys from one way of life to another. And they gift us insights that challenge lazy prejudice about Islam by providing a striking counterpoint to fears about fundamentalism, extremism, and religious hostility.

ISBN: 1 903070 392. Price £9.99

Lost Lands Forgotten Stories - Alexandra Pratt

Inspired by Mina Hubbard who made an astonishing 600 mile river journey in 1905 to restore the reputation of her late husband who had died on the same route, Alexandra Pratt retraces Hubbard's steps through the wild and ancient land of Labrador as she confronts an unforgiving landscape that surprises her at every turn.

ISBN: 1 903070 368. Price £9.99

Also by Eye Books

Jasmine and Arnica - Nicola Naylor
A blind woman's journey around India.
ISBN: 1 903070 171. Price £9.99.

Touching Tibet - Niema Ash
A journey into the heart of this intriguing forbidden kingdom.
ISBN: 1 903070 18X. Price £9.99.

Behind the Veil - Lydia Laube
A shocking account of a nurses Arabian nightmare.
ISBN: 1 903070 198. Price £9.99.

Walking Away - Charlotte Metcalf
A well known film makers African journal.
ISBN: 1 903070 201. Price £9.99.

Travels in Outback Australia - Andrew Stevenson
In search of the original Australians - the Aboriginal People.
ISBN: 1 903070 147. Price £9.99

The European Job - Jonathan Booth
10,000 miles around Europe in a 25 year old classic car.
ISBN: 1 903070 252. Price £9.99

Around the World with 1000 Birds - Russell Boyman
An extraordinary answer to a mid-life crisis.
ISBN: 1 903070 163. Price £9.99

Cry from the Highest Mountain - Tess Burrows
A climb to the point furthest from the centre of the earth.
ISBN: 1 903070 120. Price £9.99

Dancing with Sabrina - Bob Bibby
A journey from source to sea of the River Severn.
ISBN: 1 903070 244. Price £9.99

Grey Paes and Bacon - Bob Bibby
A journey around the canals of the Black Country
ISBN: 1 903070 066. Price £7.99

Jungle Janes - Peter Burden
Twelve middle-aged women take on the Jungle. As seen on Ch 4.
ISBN: 1 903070 05 8. Price £7.99

Travels with my Daughter - Niema Ash
Forget convention, follow your instincts.
ISBN: 1 903070 04 X. Price £7.99

Riding with Ghosts - Gwen Maka
One woman's solo cycle ride from Seattle to Mexico.
ISBN: 1 903070 00 7. Price £7.99

Riding with Ghosts: South of the Border - Gwen Maka
The second part of Gwen's epic cycle trip across the Americas.
ISBN: 1 903070 09 0. Price £7.99

Triumph Round the World - Robbie Marshall
He gave up his world for the freedom of the road.
ISBN: 1 903070 08 2. Price £7.99

Fever Trees of Borneo - Mark Eveleigh
A daring expedition through uncharted jungle.
ISBN: 0 953057 56 9. Price £7.99

Discovery Road - Tim Garrett and Andy Brown
Their mission was to mountain bike around the world.
ISBN: 0 953057 53 4. Price £7.99